Surviving Bill

Surviving Bill

Mike Reynolds

iUniverse, Inc.
New York Lincoln Shanghai

Surviving Bill

iUniverse books may be ordered through booksellers or by contacting:

iUniverse
2021 Pine Lake Road, Suite 100
Lincoln, NE 68512
www.iuniverse.com
1-800-Authors (1-800-288-4677)

All events in this book are true. However, the names of both people and places have been changed in most cases to protect their privacy.

ISBN-13: 978-0-595-42681-2 (pbk)
ISBN-13: 978-0-595-68223-2 (cloth)
ISBN-13: 978-0-595-87011-0 (ebk)
ISBN-10: 0-595-42681-6 (pbk)
ISBN-10: 0-595-68223-5 (cloth)
ISBN-10: 0-595-87011-2 (ebk)

Printed in the United States of America

In memory of my brother Bill

This book is dedicated to my parents whose infinite strength allowed my sisters and me to heal and thrive. I owe all that I've achieved, enjoyed and experienced to you both and I will forever be in your debt.

There is nothing in being superior to some other man
The true nobility is in being superior to your previous self.

—Hindu Proverb

Contents

Introduction

Every year, over 30,000 people commit suicide and leave behind an estimated 180,000 'survivors' who are intimately affected by their loss. As a survivor of my brother's suicide, I wrote this book to speak to them. However, I believe the elements of healing found throughout will also speak to those who've lost loved ones to almost any other circumstances as well.

◆　　　◆　　　◆

As survivors, we're the ones left behind by a family member, friend or partner to sift through the confusion, pain and rejection. We're the ones who were involuntarily designated to make sense of the most senseless thing someone could do. We're the ones who are forced to hunt for answers that will never come and to move through this dark, cold period.

While we're left with the "basic" feelings of loss—shock, denial, isolation, anger, grief and fear—we also find ourselves with a set of emotions that few of those who lose loved ones to anything but suicide experience. These include rejection, abandonment, guilt, self-recrimination, confusion, shame, and an intense fear of our loved one's surrender that we can never bring ourselves to understand.

Suicide is unique in this respect. It beats the survivor down with all that loss can create, but then strikes with a whole new set of weapons. Regardless of what's left behind—a note, a book of poems, an audio or video tape—we're left with questions that will never be answered and confusion that's constructed on the simple perplexing notion of how a person can take such a final, self-destructive step. How could they have left us, our family, children, brothers, sisters, friends—all those who are so completely dependent on their existence? What could have been so bad? Didn't they know I loved them? What did I do wrong? Did I drive them to kill themselves? Did that thing I said yesterday make them do it? Different questions arise around the method and place, the time of day or year. As survivors, we're forced to continue on, to live our lives and move beyond the towering array of emotions that infest our bodies and minds.

But how? We cry, plunge into despair and desperately cling to those closest to us. We seek out counselors, support groups and friends who are willing to hear our pain. We search for whatever answers we can find, and we try to figure out, mostly on our own, ways that we can get through each day, slowly venturing back into the world of the living. But we often don't do the one thing that could prove beneficial to our healing and other's as well—share our stories. This may be due to the shame felt from the stigma of suicide, the fear of having to explain the "why's" or the simple assumption that people just don't want to hear it. However, our existence as humans, our traditions, knowledge, beliefs and values were all derived from the communication of the common human experience. While this process allows the storyteller to learn from introspection and the exchange of perspectives that inevitably follows, it may also provide the audience with new information and ideas from which they can understand and develop their own lives and stories.

I'm not a psychologist, psychiatrist or even a suicide expert (which is one of the reasons this book isn't laden with analysis). What I do know is that I have survived the suicide of my brother Bill. I have evolved into a more confident, happy, secure, and outgoing person as a direct result of Bill's death and my management of it. I have an excellent relationship with my family and have had the good fortune of developing strong friendships and an array of romantic involvements. Of course, my life isn't perfect and every day isn't bliss. But I've been able to move significantly away from the tragedy that is Bill's death to concentrate on the triumph that is my life.

My story isn't particularly unique. In many ways it's very similar to that of countless survivors. I'm taking the time to tell it because I believe the structure I've chosen and the elements of healing on which I've honed in fill a void on the information for which survivors search. The majority of books I've found focus on the victim, the epidemic or the societal factors that create both. If books do target the survivor, they're often bogged down in clinical analysis or with the umpteenth take on the five stages of grief. They ignore the power and effect that many "ordinary" moments have throughout all of our lives. The decisions we make, synchronistic moments we experience, pivotal relationships and realizations that make up all of our healing processes are just as important as counseling or, for some, religion. These details have pushed me ahead with my healing and have made the difference in allowing me to become who I am. Hopefully, my story will help you identify your own.

My journey begins with the day before Bill's suicide and ends with my life now. Beyond the descriptions of the days following Bill's death, all I have concentrated on are those moments that have moved my healing forward. The moments are presented purely for what transpired. I left out any interpretation so as not to cloud your own specific application. My moments include the introduction of Death, increased insight into why Bill took his own life, the instances when Bill came back to me, my places of safety and refuge, the construction of my "enlightened" perspective, counseling, my relationships and brushes with my own mortality. In their own ways, these instances propelled me towards the social, positive and self-assured person I am now.

The progression in my healing, however, couldn't have occurred if not for one basic principle instilled in me by my family, in particular, my mother. Through her own example and loving, persistent prodding, she made us clearly see that our lives didn't end with Bill's. While we undoubtedly experienced one of the most horrid tragedies imaginable, we couldn't shut down and wither away. We had to stay open to all that life offered, to learn the new exciting things that would always stoke the fire within our hearts, to live life in every way we could possibly imagine. She refused to lose the rest of her family as she had lost Bill. As a result, I was able to welcome each moment described throughout this book. It's this idea that's at the heart of all that you'll read. And it's this idea that I beg you to keep at the forefront of your mind in order to move your own life forward.

I hope you find solace and camaraderie throughout this book, and I hope your journey leads you to the same wonderful place that mine has led me.

1

It was Sunday, May 4, and the day seemed to foreshadow another summer of the shore, baseball, t-shirts and fun. Unfortunately, my brother Bill and I had been summoned to partake in that favorite pastime common to all fathers—manual labor. Bill and I had been given the task of watering the eleven pine trees he had just planted across the front yard. They were supposed to provide a barrier to the new neighbor's house, but at the time were only a foot high. It had taken Bill several weekends to dig the holes and haul the saplings across the yard, lifting and placing them just right so that they stood strong and straight and according to my father's plan, he still had nine more trees to plant. I'm sure Bill felt that the project would never end.

The day had been long and arduous, filled from the early morning with weeding, raking, fertilizing and picking up the bush clippings my father left behind as he snipped away with his shears. After all those chores, watering the small trees seemed like a piece of cake. Bill (15) dragged the hose down to the small saplings while I (10) held onto the slack. Reaching them, we crouched down like two catchers waiting for a pitch and began to water their bases. Exhausted, we were tapping into the last bit of energy left from our long day as lawn boys, when Bill suddenly got a shine in his eyes and said, "Hey, you wanna build a volcano?"

"Sure," I said not really knowing what in the world he was talking about.

At that, Bill stuck the nozzle into the bottom of the mound of dirt. His arm disappeared up to his elbow; a smirk supported a gleam that started to fill his eyes with anticipation. Instantaneously, a deep rumble rose from inside the earth. The dirt shuddered as the sound began to grow with a moan and steady powerful surge. "Lean in," he said. "You need to come in close to see this." Small rocks and soil from the top of the mound started to fall away, tumbling to the bottom of the pile. Then, from my brilliant vantage point of six inches, I witnessed the full fury and eruption of Mt. Bill as it blew off the top mound of earth, spewing water, rocks, grubs and dirt all over me.

"Whoooooaaaaaaaaa!" I yelled, falling back onto my heels. "That was way cool!"

Bill rolled on the ground laughing hysterically, thinking, 'How can he keep falling for this stuff!' Amazed at the spectacle that unfolded before me and not caring how dirty I'd gotten, I begged Bill to do it again. But just as quickly as Mt. Bill blasted out Queen Anne Court, the show was brought to a grinding halt as my father ordered us to finish watering the trees, wrap up the hose and gather and clean off the tools that lay strewn around every corner of our yard. Murmuring our discontent, Bill and I stood up and set out to finish the rest of the tasks.

I don't know if it was our exhaustion or just having spent too much time together, but while Bill and I gathered up the tools, we got into some stupid disagreement about some meaningless thing that grew into a full-on argument—the kind that all brothers at that age have almost every day of their lives. We shouted at each other, called each other names and both blamed the other for God knows what. Finally the whole argument ended when I shouted, "I WISH YOU WERE DEAD!" At the time, I had no idea how prophetic those words would be.

2

The following day passed like any other. I went to school, pitched in my Little League game, went home, ate and did my homework. And like every other day, I desperately tried to extend my bedtime. Typically, I watched television in the back of the family room, hoping my parents would forget I was there, or milk a huge bowl of ice cream, trying to make it last an extra half hour. But, as usual, I was denied and told to go up at 9:30. Dressed in my T-shirt and tighty-whities, I begrudgingly went up the stairs to the room that Bill and I shared.

Bill had already been up there doing homework and as usual the door was closed. Strangely though, this time the door was locked. I knocked and asked Bill to open up. Nothing.

"Come on, Bill. I have to go to bed!" I yelled. Nothing.

"Bill, stop screwing around. Come on! Open the door!" No response.

"I'm gonna get Mom and Dad!" I exclaimed as my last threat. But the door didn't swing open nor did a voice come from behind it.

Still figuring Bill just didn't want to deal with me, I marched downstairs yelling, "Moooom! Daaaaaaaad! Bill won't open the door." Finding them both in the family room, I went in and explained the situation to them. My father muttered "Jeezus" under his breath and they both went upstairs with me trailing behind.

My father knocked on the door and told Bill to open up. Still there was nothing.

"Let's go Bill!" He yelled.

Nothing.

As he has since told me, an intense, dark feeling ripped through my father. He began to throw his large 6'4" frame against the door to break it down. There was still no sound from Bill and the only noise came from the wood in the door jamb as it began to stretch and crack. My sisters both came out of their rooms to see the source of the commotion and, on his second or third try, we saw my father blast the door into small fragments of wood that blew onto Bill's empty bed.

My father ran in. I cautiously followed, only to be swept backwards when he yelled, "Get Michael out of here!" Somebody pulled me back and all I remember are flashes of the ceiling, the splintered door, the blue carpeting in the hallway, the side of my sister Suzanne's head and the blur as my mother ran by. Just before I was led downstairs, I heard my father say, "GET THE ROPE!" and I knew what had happened.

My father recently told me that when he entered the room he scanned every corner and didn't see anything except that the huge walk-in closet's door lay open with the light on. He ran over, looked in and saw Bill half standing, hunched over like a rag doll, with a necktie that wrapped around his neck and stretched to the clothes rack that lined the back of our closet. He ripped off the noose, put Bill on the floor and tried to administer CPR. With no response, he just pounded on Bill's chest and yelled.

With his feet still on the ground, Bill had cut off his air supply by tying the tie around his neck and leaning forward. The noose rested just under his chin and according to the coroner, almost immediately cut off his breathing. There was essentially no turning back once Bill leaned forward. He quickly lost consciousness and, soon thereafter, his life.

Then … everyone was there; the police, paramedics and the neighbors. I was downstairs, not comprehending all that was happening around me. Paralyzed on the couch, I became transfixed, staring at my neighbor, Mrs. Thompson. Out of nowhere, a rush filled the doorway as several paramedics flew by carrying Bill on a stretcher with a sheet covering his entire body. No one had said much to me at that point about what was happening, but with that sight, I just knew. Looking back and forth from the now empty doorway and Mrs. Thompson, I started yelling, "HE CAN'T DIE! HE'S MY BROTHER! HE CAN'T DIE! THERE'S NO WAY! HE'S MY BROTHER! HE CAN'T DIE!"

The fact that Bill could be dead was inconceivable. He had always been my protector, confidant and inspiration. He sat up with me late at night, explaining how to protect myself against the bullies in school and was the one who confronted them if they kept up their abuse. He advised me on the matters of love, drawing from his own experience to counsel me on the smoothest way to approach that girl I'd been eyeing from the back of math class. He was my biggest source of pride when he tackled someone on the football field or knocked out another home run. He was the ultimate adversary in our games of war (he would always insist that our shots missed him!) or in our mud and snowball fights. In the spring, summer and fall, we rode our bikes together and took long exploratory hikes through the 300 acres of woods and fields that bordered our property. In the winter, we set up incredible sled runs down the huge hill we had next to the house in which we lived growing up. He even showed me how to feign sleeping when my mother would come in to wake us for Sunday school and the expression to possess to sway her in allowing us to sleep in. Of course, we got into your normal brother squabbles, but even then I knew he loved me. For Bill to die … no … it just wasn't possible. When he passed by on the stretcher, I knew right then in my heart that he was either gone or close to it. Yet I still tried to hang on to the hope of some possibility that he was okay.

The next thing I remember is going back upstairs, to our bedroom, to put on a pair of pants. I sheepishly entered the room and noticed the door in pieces against the side wall and the abundant number of emergency people. The paramedics were putting their supplies away and the police were combing through our drawers and clothes, coming in and out of the closet and taking notes. It looked like the hustle and bustle you'd see at a crime scene and I remember wondering what they were looking for, if Bill did something wrong, if he was in trouble, if I was in the way, why they weren't just helping Bill rather than ripping our stuff apart.

When they noticed me, every eye filled with horror and instinctually shot towards the floor. No one looked directly at me, but rather peered sideways over notebooks or medical bags. They had no idea what I knew or what to say, but they needn't say a word.

My father had gone with the paramedics to the hospital and much to my dismay returned shortly thereafter—without Bill. "Where was he?" "Is he okay?" "What happened?" were the questions we all had filling our heads. It took him awhile to walk down our front walk, but once he got close, we noticed even in the darkness that he looked ashen, exhausted and had obviously been crying. This 225 pound man looked somehow smaller, frail and weak. He sat us all down on the front step. My heart sank as I had never seen my father so nervous. One police car still sat in our court with its lights slowly working their way around the neighborhood. Each house, car, tree, yard and driveway within view became rhythmically awash in a flash of red light so that the wide expanding glow could be followed around and around and around. Finally, with all of the energy he could muster, he told us that Bill wouldn't be coming home, that he had a heart attack and just didn't make it. I thought about the rope comment and knew that Bill had not died the way my father was telling us, but didn't question him. I came to learn much later that everyone in my family had known what Bill had done. They just couldn't imagine that I'd be able to handle the concept of suicide at ten.

I kept thinking that none of this could actually be happening. I longingly watched the street that rose up to our house and hoped that I would see Bill running up it yelling, "Hey, everybody. I'm sorry. I'm right here. I just needed to get away for a little while. I really screwed up. Sorry about that." I remember also thinking that maybe he bribed the doctors to tell my father he was dead so he could get away from us. That would've been okay, because he would still be alive and I could always find him. But the more my father spoke, the more real it all became. My older, vibrant, virile, stronger brother was gone.

And then it happened.

Before my eyes, death rose from something abstract and mysterious to become a tangible, real being that could be touched and tasted and smelled as easily as Mom's apple pie on Thanksgiving. Formless stature and invisibility allowed Him to infiltrate every corner of our house, yard and woods that surrounded our once-protected adolescent Eden. He came back from the hospital with my father, settling down among us, as my father explained to his wife and three remaining children what happened to Bill. Death enjoyed this moment of our pain I thought, and I could feel His laughter mocking us, as He took pleasure in the fact that He had gotten another and a young one at that.

As my father spoke I gazed out at the huge expanse of yards that opened up beyond our property line. The sky, a deep foreboding midnight blue, contrasted sharply with scenery whose color was quickly seeping out of every pore. Our neighbor's trees, house and cars had all been consumed by black. The pine trees that Bill had planted across the yard still shone green, but a much deeper shade. Even the brick stairs below my feet appeared to suck in the blackness of the tragedy that pressed down upon us.

But it wasn't just the darkness closing in that I noticed the most. Everything now looked different. The neighbor's yard, those puny pine trees and even the brick just looked different. The grass, the driveway, the people in front of me whom I had grown up with. My hands, feet, shoes, pants and even the cesspool that obnoxiously rose above the right corner of our yard all looked like they hadn't before. They looked, I realized, impermanent. All of those things could be gone, wiped away, obliterated in just a moment. They, like Bill, could die and what I saw then in front of me would, no doubt, change by morning and then again by midday and again by next month. Immediately, I knew that nothing on which I gazed, including my own body, could escape Death.

This is also when the smell struck me. It was that smell that would appear only on those summer nights when the air was heavy with heat and the scents of the trees, flowers, grass, dirt and rock all compressed together. Before that night, I had always enjoyed that smell, as it signified the coming of summer, the ending of school and the time of the year when I could play touch football or basketball until eight at night. But on that evening, it became the aroma of death.

My father continued talking and then answered our questions, which must have been brutal for him. After awhile, we all just sat there, cried and held each other, overwrought with complete disbelief and grief.

From the point after my father spoke to us, the rest of the night is a blur. I do remember feeling more exhausted, weak and frightened than I ever had in my entire life. As Death enveloped our house, fear that I would succumb to His grasp, as had my brother only a few hours before, filled my mind. I became acutely aware of every breath, heartbeat and moment that passed; reveling in each minute I foiled His plans to take me away too. I couldn't be alone and clung to my parents and sisters.

At some point, I had to go to bed. For the first time, this became a harrowing thought. No way could I sleep in the room that Bill and I shared. The emotions that swept over me earlier in the evening when I went to get my pajama bottoms were bad enough. Now, everything was infinitely magnified. If Death felt comfortable anywhere in that house, it had to be there. Furthermore, I had to close my eyes and turn out the light, which exposed me to Death like an injured antelope lying down in front of a lion. Without me saying a word, my parents set up a cot at the foot of their bed. I felt safer there, but still as though Death was standing at my side, laughing at my fear. All I wanted was to sleep peacefully and wake to the sight of the sun blasting through the blinds.

3

I woke that first morning and, for a split second, felt fantastic. The day blazed with an early summer morning's heat and I was excited for what it held in store. I began to think about what I'd do and then—WHAMMM! My world shattered again when the realization violently swept over me that Bill had died the night before. My brother was gone forever. I felt my exhaustion from crying all night and my eyes were swollen and heavy. The fear of dying, sadness and a deep wish that what was real was not all hung in the air, as though a smog of misery had overtaken the house. I was so glad to be alive and to see the sunshine streaming through the blinds, but was petrified to move. Where would I be safest? On the cot? In my parents' room? Outside, away from this house? Oh God, I just didn't know what to do, where to look, what to say. I cried and cried and cried and decided that the best thing I could do was to find my family. I sprang off the cot and out of my parents' room, through the hallway, past the shattered fragments of wood leaning against the door frame and down the stairs. I found my family in the kitchen talking on the phone to neighbors, priests and colleagues. They looked swollen with pain, weak, withered and numb.

Fear pulsed through my blood. Death was real now. It sat next to us the night before on the stairs, slept with me in my cot, emanated from the room Bill and I shared and floated over everyone and everything in that house. In one night, I went from an adolescent who knew he would live forever to one that just hoped to make it through the next few hours. Nothing was sure with Death begging for the chance to suck the life out of my small skinny body.

And Bill. My God I ached for Bill. I didn't think a lot about what he did; I just crumbled at the thought that he was gone. I thought of the words I spoke to him the previous afternoon and wondered aloud to myself if they drove him over the edge. I begged to know why he would want to leave me, us, this world. I froze when I pictured all the ways he had helped me—learning how to fight, catch a ball, ride a bike—and couldn't imagine how I'd do it all on my own. I wasn't angry at him. I just wanted him back. Where was he? Was he really dead? What exactly does that *mean*? My world was gone and instantly, I felt … not of this world. I had seen death in my brother's lifeless body as it was carried away through my house and the effect it had on my sisters, mother and father in both physical and mental ways. They had been drawn and quartered into hollow shells of themselves and I knew that I appeared the same way. Life was no longer about living. For that day and for the weeks and months to come, life felt like it was just to avoid Death.

4

Somehow, my parents moved through the next few days and organized the funeral. The services took place at a huge white funeral home that stood along the country road that took Bill to school every day. Hundreds of people lined up outside the door and far down the street. They were friends, neighbors, my parents' colleagues and complete strangers who could only imagine the tragedy that had befallen my family.

Wanting to shield me from the intense sorrow, my parents encouraged me to spend most of my time in the back rooms of the funeral home, far away from the continuous procession of mourners. I cried a bit, but mostly just walked around feeling numb and cold. One of the funeral directors had no idea what to do with me and so took me on a tour. He avoided the embalming rooms, thank God, but did show me where they kept the caskets. I recall when he opened the door, I thought, "Pal, this is the last thing I wanna look at!" But I knew he was trying his best to keep me occupied and, for that, I gave him credit.

Toward the end of the services, my mother found me and asked that I come with her to the parlor. Our family, she explained, was going to say a final goodbye to Bill. With overwhelming dread, I cried while I took my mother's hand and we wound our way out of the safe havens of the back rooms into the viewing. I don't recall much about the room or the people who were there, but I do remember desperately not wanting to go up and see Bill lying there. I was so scared. Of what, I'm not exactly sure. My family gathered together, we all held hands, walked across the room and stood alongside the casket. I looked at him as little as possible, unable to bear the sight before me. The person lying there with his eyes closed, hands folded, wearing a suit and tie and with thick swaths of make-up on his blood-drained, beige skin wasn't the older brother I grew up with, played and joked with just a few days before. His energy, spirit and voice were so far gone from the shell that lay before me. But the moment did serve as confirmation for me that Bill was dead, arresting my disbelief and desired denial.

After a long day of despair and fear, Bill's body was lowered into the ground at Our Lady of the Mountain church, covered and marked with a nondescript, flat stone that held a simple brass plate which reads:

William John Reynolds

"Our Bill"

December 4, 1964   May 5, 1980

5

So, of course, the big question you're asking is "WHY?" Why would such a fun, healthy, loved young boy from a good family cunningly tie a noose around his neck and kill himself? Was he on drugs? No. Was he depressed? Nobody thought so. Did he give a sign that he was so at the end of the road of choices that suicide was the only "logical" one for him? Absolutely not.

In the first few days and weeks following Bill's death, my family was as blindsided as one whose child had been murdered. We couldn't fathom why he would take such a step.

The only clue Bill left behind was a book of poems placed on his bed entitled, "The Best Loved Poems of the American People," in which he marked certain works with a red dot, a strip of paper or both. But as you can see in the back of this book, the poems offered no explanations, only solace and comfort to those left behind. The poems Bill chose spoke of God's beauty, evidence of immortality in nature, ruminations on why we suffer, the longing of a brother who has lost his older one and the idea that death is actually a beginning not an end. Bill seemed to implore us to be happy for him and to rest easy with the thoughts that, as one poem he chose stated, "He is not dead. He is just away."

But as the sting from the initial blow of his death began to subside, my parents turned their energies to racking their minds for reasons. And over the next several days, three memories burst forth that at least provided a glimpse.

Since the public school was overwrought with drugs at the time, my parents decided to send him to Smith Roberts, a private school four towns away. They thought it offered a safe haven from the drugs and a solid education. The students appeared to be upper-middle class, the campus was nice and the athletic programs, in which Bill would participate, were strong and well supported. His grades were good during the year, as were his spirits, and he did well with the clubs and sports in which he was involved. Most of the time passed without as much as a blip. But in the few months before his death, Bill began to reach out.

The first incident poked forth when Bill talked about quitting the wrestling team. The incessant dieting and seriousness with which they approached an activity that was supposed to be fun wore him down. Wrestling wasn't the outlet he had hoped for. When my father suggested he quit, Bill insisted that he couldn't as the coach and his teammates had already been harassing him for even thinking about it. The promise of physical harm rained down on him if he left the team, and signs reading "Quitter" were posted on his locker. He felt the only thing he could do was to ride out the year. My father asked him if he could take the pressure until then and Bill assured him that he could. With his son's conviction strong, my father felt he had little to worry about.

Bill also approached my sister Suzanne about a month before he died, telling her of the overwhelming presence of drugs in Smith Roberts. It was the first time he had mentioned drugs to anyone and she was shocked. He told her that he wasn't using, but their presence was so large that he increasingly became an outsider at school. Kids called him a "nark" and one went so far as to say, "If you're not doing drugs now, then you're gonna be on them by junior year. So, you might as well start." He didn't know what to do. He felt as though he couldn't drop out since my parents spent so much on his tuition and the year was almost over. When Suzanne begged Bill to talk to our parents, he refused and said he "would handle it," insisting that she not mention the conversation to them.

Worried, Suzanne went to my parents anyway. They called Bill in that night and asked him what was going on. He acknowledged the prevalence of drugs at Smith Roberts, but greatly downplayed their severity. Again, he convincingly told them that he could handle the situation and never mentioned his desire to leave school. After what my parents felt was an open and productive conversation, they were confident in the advice they gave him on how to continue to avoid drugs and the assurance that he could always come to them if things got worse.

The only other time Bill gave any indication of his pain was on the morning of the day he died. For some reason, my father drove Bill to school rather than have him take the bus. During the ride, Bill asked my father about the possibility of switching schools. My father assured him that it would be fine, but asked if he could just ride out the next few weeks, since the year was almost over. They could decide on where he wanted to go in the summer. Bill agreed and dropped the whole issue. When they arrived at the school, my father offered to walk in with him, but he became agitated and adamantly said "No!"

After school that day, my father and Bill came to watch my Little League baseball game. Bill was noticeably irritable and upset. When my father asked him what was wrong and could they talk, Bill said no and stormed off, sitting high up on a steep gravelly ledge that overlooked the left field line. Figuring Bill just needed some time alone to cool down from some adolescent fit, my father let him be.

The game ended, we all drove home and Bill seemed to be fine. We got home at 8:30. He went upstairs at 9:00 to do homework and by 9:30 he was dead.

As they say, hindsight is 20/20 and, undoubtedly, the above instances were all cries for help. But these instances were the only ones in which Bill expressed to us any level of fear, urgency and pain. What he gave my sister and father were mere glimpses at the depths of his despair. He let them into his misery only so far and it was clearly not enough to let them understand just how bad things were for him.

The depths of the hardships with which Bill was dealing were slowly unveiled to our family through the multitude of people who came to his funeral and to our house in the weeks that followed. They boldly told their stories of Bill and painted a vivid picture of the school in a desperate attempt to help us to understand why he did what he did. Fellow students, parents and even his bus driver made a point of trying to fill in the many gaps that plagued us.

Students described the student body as rich kids expelled from other schools and inner-city kids bused to Smith Roberts when their high school had closed down. Together, these two groups created an "Animal House" type of environment where drugs were openly used and sold, school property often vandalized and disorderly conduct rarely punished by a faculty who were mostly screwed up themselves. Bill, they told us, was one of the few kids to hold out against drugs and, as a result, copped an inordinate amount of abuse. They wanted my parents to know that Bill wasn't like most of the other kids. He was clean, kind and, because of that, the brunt of their excessive abuse. The scene described represented the antithesis of what my parents had thought it was. Unknowingly, they sent their eldest son into the lion's den.

Several days after the funeral, Bill's bus driver came to the house saying that he felt compelled to relay the following story: For a long time many of the football players and wrestlers on the bus badgered and beat up on a much smaller and weaker kid. The harassment carried on for quite some time until one day Bill couldn't take it any longer. He stood up in front of the bus and announced that if anybody wanted to bully this kid, they would have to go through him first. Silence overtook the vehicle and Bill found himself looking upon a legion of stunned faces. Satisfied, Bill sat down next to the kid and did so every day forward. The weaker kid was never bothered again, but I suspect the move only served to further alienate Bill from the abusive student body.

With the newfound knowledge offered by these and many other stories, my parents came to the understanding that Bill died because he was a good kid. He died because he didn't do drugs, because he cared about other people, because he had a warm heart and an old soul. My sister, Colleen, put it best when she said, "Bill was too much for this world in the sense that he was overly sensitive to the wrongs done to him and to other people. He took everything to heart and felt that he, alone, should be able to find the solutions to all of his and the world's problems. He simply felt too much."

But as tempting as it is to paint this reasoning for Bill's suicide, it's clearly not the whole story. For a long time, I thought it was. I thought the environment at Smith Roberts, the pressure exerted on Bill from the other students and the faculty, even the sensitive and caring way with which Bill saw the world were enough to cause him to take his own life. While these were all factors that contributed to his suicide, I found out through extensive research that there was probably much more going on inside him that was as equally destructive.

In her excellent, comprehensive book entitled, *Night Falls Fast: Understanding Suicide*, Kay Redfield Jamison notes that while most people encounter difficult situations throughout life (i.e. loss, divorce, financial ruin), very few commit suicide. The real factor that causes suicidal victims to take that extra step of killing themselves is mental illness. Usually, this takes the form of depression, which is a physiological chemical (serotonin) deficiency in the body, but it can also consist of schizophrenia, manic depression and other such conditions. Mental illness can be measured and witnessed in an overwhelming majority of suicidal people. In fact, countless studies estimate that mental illness is present in 90–95 percent of suicide victims (*Night Falls Fast: Understanding Suicide*). People just don't decide to take their own lives when their brains are working in a normal capacity.

Ms. Redfield Jamison also notes however, that tragic or emotionally debilitating events may cause the serotonin levels to drop, initiating depression. I found this particular point interesting, as it highlighted the fact that the pressure from the students and faculty at Smith Roberts could have caused Bill's depression. While the events alone are not enough to have caused Bill to take his own life, they could have created the physiological changes in Bill's brain which would have incapacitated his reasoning abilities. Furthermore, my family has also wondered if the severe drop in weight to qualify for his wrestling matches may have also caused his serotonin levels to drop, but I was unable to locate any research supporting this.

At 15, Bill was inadvertently thrust into a sadistic environment that, no matter how you look at it, caused his mind to break down. Death became for him, not just an end, but a preferred solution to escape something he viewed as inescapable. I can't fathom what jumbled, confusing thoughts rifled through my wonderful brother's mind, all the while our family thought he was doing fine. It's true that he saw the world differently than most. But it was probably not just with sympathetic, sensitive eyes. It was most likely a world viewed through cloudy and frightening confusion.

My mother recently pulled an article that she had saved in her 'Bill' file that provided even more insight into why he committed suicide when he did. It was from *The Star Ledger* newspaper on January 17, 1984—four years after Bill died. It outlined the findings of a study conducted by Kathleen MacMahon at the Harvard School of Public Health and was based on an analysis of 185,887 suicides in the U.S. from 1972–1978. The study confirmed three key details of my experience: Monday is the most common day for suicides, May is the most common month and the 5th of the month is the peak for suicides. Bill's death fulfilled all three components. No one is sure why these details factor into the equation of suicide. Regarding the time of year, some speculate that the contrast between depression and the annual springtime rebirth of nature only enhances the sadness that the person feels and plunges them further into their depression. It's also speculated that springtime energizes depressed persons enough to give them the strength to finally carry through with their deadly wishes.

6

During the days and weeks that followed, I wandered around the house in a constant daze, racked by exhaustion. A haze clouded everything on which I looked, created by my tears or their residue. It took all my energy to drag my body from point to point, feeling as though cement blocks were fastened to my feet. Nothing felt real, like I was trapped within a horrible dream. I hated being in the house where Bill died and Death now freely wandered. Death poured from every wall, doorway and dark corner of every room. I felt helplessly enveloped within His immeasurable power and overwhelming dominance. Yet, our house was the only place I could ever fathom being. I didn't ever want to leave it and couldn't imagine things like school or playing with the other kids. There were days when my body felt hollow, as though everything—my bones, heart, mind, lungs, muscles—had been scooped out to leave just an outside shell and it would only take a breeze to destroy me.

There were moments amidst this maelstrom of fear, however, that Death became alluring, drawing me in to commit suicide. At these times, Death appeared to shed its foreboding, evil shell and don all things sensual, peaceful and beautiful, attempting to gently coerce me to allow Him to take me away to the place He had taken Bill. "You and Bill would be together again," Death whispered in my ear. "You'll feel better. You'll feel at ease. You'll feel … happy."

Death wasn't something I wanted as an escape from my sadness or depression. It simply felt easy. Part of it was that I missed Bill and knowing where he'd gone would have provided untold answers. But part of it too revolved around the idea that, for so long, death had been an abstract notion, something always wrapped in a package of intrigue and mystery. Suddenly, death became real and was this being I could touch, taste and smell. It became something that if I wanted to, I'd be able to wrap my arms around it like a loved one or a pet. All I had to do was repeat Bill's simple, painless actions.

Several things prevented me from taking that extra step over the edge. First, I knew the emotional ruin that Bill's death had on me and I couldn't imagine doing that to anyone in my family again. Second, I knew, even then, that what

Bill did was wrong. At this point, I didn't know the issues that forced him to make his tragic decision, but nothing could justify Bill leaving me here alone, mentally and physically destroyed. Finally, every day since Bill had died, I thought about the fact that he'd never see the sun set; the smooth breaking waves at the shore; a smile; the deer; or even our dog, Barney, again. I enjoyed these things and wasn't ready to let them go.

Make no mistake, each time Death attempted to woo me into following Bill, I dug my feet into the sand to restrain against the temptations of *just dying*. The moments made me shudder, and I'd stop whatever I was doing to decide whether I really wanted to go away for good. No matter where I stood, I closed my eyes and asked myself if this moment was where I wanted it to end. It was as easy as drinking a Coke or walking and I battled *not* to do it.

My sisters and I stayed out of school for two weeks while my father stayed home from work for one and a half. Not only did I fear being unable to stop crying, but I also couldn't bear the thought of walking into a classroom full of kids who couldn't possibly have any idea what I was feeling. My mother, however, refused to allow us to crumble and forced each of us to take the initial crucial step of getting on with our lives. The enormity of her strength resided in the fact that in getting us all out of the house, she was forced to spend the majority of her days alone with only time to contemplate what had happened with her son, why and what could have been done. I don't remember her ever not being strong and realize now the toll that must have taken. But she was the foundation of our family at the time and the inspiring example of what we had to do. We couldn't wallow in misery and pain. We could cry, miss Bill, and even crumble to the floor when those moments of reality hit us across the face. But we weren't allowed to just wither away and let Bill's death make our desire for life pass us by. My mother put the power and the decision to heal into each of our own hands. With that initial push out the door, back into the world, she showed us that we had the strength to get through this. It would be the toughest thing we ever dealt with, but there was more out there to do and to see. Our life didn't end with Bill's death.

My mother's prodding represented the crossroads of our healing. In that period, we survivors make our decision to either live or die psychologically. If we choose the former, we learn to use our terrible experience to strengthen our hearts and minds. If we choose the latter, then we become one of those people who wear pain about their face like a huge bruise for the entire world to see, whose attitude towards life is that it owes them something and who often try to find solace in substance abuse or other forms of self-destruction. In many ways, these people have died with their loved ones and life becomes nothing more than hardship and misery.

Walking into school after all that transpired in the previous weeks was like walking naked down the center of a busy street. I could feel every eye fixed on me and became self-conscious that I was the kid whose brother died. When I walked into a classroom, silence fell across the room like a wave rolling through from my feet to the far wall. Some kids looked afraid of me, while others looked with consolation. Only a few said anything to me about Bill and most of those were "Sorry 'bout your brother," after which they would quickly change the subject or turn away. Constantly fearful of crying, I became petrified of moments when something would remind me of Bill. Movies like "Old Yeller" and readings from such books as "The Red Fern" were deeply stressful situations. When I couldn't take them, I'd quietly leave the room, shake off the teacher's inquiry of where I was going and escape into a stall in the bathroom to bawl my eyes out.

Outside of school, I spent a lot of time by myself: shooting baskets in the driveway, walking in the woods with my dog, or just throwing a football as far as I could in the backyard with no one there to catch it. I couldn't bear talking to the other kids any more than I had to and wanted to withdraw from everyone but my family. I constantly thought about Bill, his death and what lie in store for me. Questions incessantly rifled through my head such as: Who *am* I? Where's Bill? What's important? What should I focus on now? Will I ever find my way out of this pain? What's going to happen to Mom, Dad, Colleen, Suzanne? Is Bill really dead? Is there a God? If there is a God, what is His justification for taking Bill? I hated God, the church, the situation in which Bill had thrust me, the fact that Bill was gone. I hated the pain I always felt and I hated how unreachable it was, residing deep inside my body.

Everything became so complicated—intertwined in mystery, abstraction and pain. Always there was some amount of pain. Life had to be simpler than this, I reasoned, and this simplicity was all for which I longed.

During this period, I remember becoming fascinated with an ad for Parliament cigarettes that I ripped out of a magazine and taped to my bedroom wall. It showed a couple lying on the sand of a small deserted island in bathing suits with their boat beached nearby. The island itself resembled more of an atoll, rising only six feet out of the water and perfectly round. In the center sat a cluster of a half dozen palm trees whose bases were covered in a thick green scrub. Sand covered most of the area and shone so white that you may have thought it snow had you not been in the center of the tropics. Minute waves caressingly lapped the shore, stroking the man's toes. The blue/green reef, just off the beach, lie clearly visible through the translucent teal water and stretched out towards the horizon until it dropped off into the deep, dark, open ocean. It was easy to imagine nothing else around for thousands of miles. No people, buildings or sadness for as far as the eye could see. The picture was all for which I longed—simplicity and a heart unbridled from pain, hurt and horror. I used to stare at the picture for long periods, thinking how wonderful it would be to stow away forever on its tiny confines. To somehow live off the land and sea until the day I died.

As if out of a need to confirm my desires, I once brought the picture down to my father and said, "Hey, Dad! Check this out! Does this not look perfect? Some day I'm gonna save up all my money, quit my job and move to an island just like this forever. Wouldn't that be awesome?" My tone was forcibly excited, as I was intent on selling him on the idea. I can vividly see him glancing at the picture and almost instantaneously responding, "Honestly? Well, no it doesn't look that great. I mean, yeah, it's a nice island. But, wouldn't you get lonely? Wouldn't you get bored after awhile? Don't you want to do more? Wouldn't you miss all of us? When would we get to see ya?" And I knew he was right. I knew right then, standing there, clutching my plan for escaping the emotional hell I felt trapped within, that island was not the answer. But, for a time, the idealistic simplicity won out over reason.

I continued in this vein for a couple of months during which my good friend and neighbor, Scott would call periodically to see if I wanted to play. I usually ignored his calls or just told my mother that I wasn't up for it. While she was cognizant of the fact that I had to get out and interact with people, I think she sensed that I needed to feel ready for this next step.

Finally, one day, when I must have just hit my limit of loneliness and solitude, I reluctantly took his phone call and agreed to go over to his house. The walk through the various backyards loomed ahead of me as I imagine the hallway does in a prison to someone walking to his execution. I dreaded our conversation and the questions Scott would ask about Bill. He couldn't understand anything I felt and no amount of explanation could paint a clear picture of the pain coursing through my mind and heart. I just wanted to play.

I remember shaking as I stood on his doorstep with my finger on the doorbell. I wanted to run back home and do this some other day, but before I could leave, the door opened. Scott stood there with a smile on his face and said, "Hey, Mike. Come on in. It's been a while."

"I know," I said, "I … I haven't been feelin' great …"

"That's okay—come on in," Scott said.

I don't remember what we talked about, but I remember that it was nothing about Bill or his death. I recall thinking Scott must have been briefed on what not to say to me, and I was so thankful.

Scott's warm welcome helped me to understand that I could get back to spending time with the other kids again and wouldn't be inundated with horrendous, curious questions about Bill. I still took my integration back into the neighborhood games slowly, but the point was, I took it. I was relieved to find though, for the most part, that everyone was very understanding. Of course, there were those moments when some kid would say, "Your brother was stupid" or "You're the one with the dumb dead brother" and I would either walk away upset or start throwing punches. But those times were rare. I had to take those initial steps back into the world and that one simple day with Scott pushed me just another step closer to getting through the pain and horror that had become my life.

7

During this period, I was never angry with Bill for taking his life. I just missed him terribly. I remember being willing to do anything to bring him back to us, even bargaining with God. I tried to negotiate with Him, thinking such things as, "You can take me in a couple of years, but just bring him back to us now." Many times a day, I stood in front of the huge bay windows that stretched almost the entire length of our living room, staring across the front yard, hoping for a glimpse of Bill walking up our street towards our house. I practiced what I would say to him and how I would say it. Bringing him up into our room and sitting him down on his bed, I would tell him I loved him and how important he was to me and our family. Our family wasn't *our family* without him and we could only function if he were a part of it. I'd apologize for what I had said the day before he died and urge him to come to me with any problems he had in the future and to never, ever take his life again.

The parish priests were the only people with whom I did become angry. Since I had no access to God personally, I vented about the injustice of taking my 15-year old brother on those next in line. Furthermore, I recalled sermons in church denouncing those who had committed suicide as condemned to Hell, and that was too much to bear.

The priests came to our house often in the months following Bill's suicide, and I wanted nothing to do with them. I remember one night in particular when Father George, our pastor, stopped by. I lay upstairs in my parents' bed watching television when my sister Colleen came in asking if I would like to see him. Becoming immediately incensed, I started screaming, "No! He's a sucker! Tell him he's a sucker!" It was the worst word I knew at the time and I yelled it hoping Father George would feel my hatred to the bottom of his heart. I steamed in bed that night with the thoughts of how much I hated God and the priests who espoused his teachings. They had never spent so much time with my family before and it was too little too late.

My parents still brought me to church every Sunday and I attended CCD when I didn't succeed in the "Pretending to Sleep" scam. I never challenged the priests or teachers directly, but rather simply spent the hour thinking about other things. After many months, I gradually learned of the support that the priests did in fact give to my parents and their efforts to quickly erase the notion that Bill's suicide was a sin. Reaching the understanding that priests were simply human beings who devoted their time to an uncompromising worship of their faith, I realized that they didn't deserve my scorn. Over time, my anger subsided with them to the point where I rarely considered it.

8

For the first time in my life, I also felt enlightened. I had always known a great deal of happiness, but now through Bill's death, I had become exposed to ultimate sadness. My span of understanding the levels of emotions one can feel soared exponentially. I had slept, ate and walked with Death and survived. Nothing could ever frighten me again. I felt I knew the secrets of life and that I alone possessed them. Whether walking through the woods, down the street or through the school hallways, these new feelings of empowerment gave me the sensation of floating above everyone else. I was above them because their lives were plain and stable. Above them, because up to now, they had known only contentment. Above them, because at most disappointment for them meant a 'C' on a test or the loss of a pet. Without the type of experience that I had gone through, I believed they could have no concept of what life meant or what really mattered.

Though I offered no answers, I felt in my heart that I now held the ability to begin to understand what was and wasn't important and to see the world around me in just those terms. When I looked at the things that people strove to do and to possess and to see, it all appeared so superfluous. People built their lives around making more money, driving faster, sleeker cars and building their dream house. I heard the kids in school exclaiming that "Jimmy got the coolest bike" or "Susie isn't cool to talk to," and I couldn't have cared less. I whittled the importance of life down to family and happiness. In school, I was only like the other kids in age and body. But the air I breathed, the view from my eyes and the sounds that drifted into my ears were all different from what those around me experienced.

Although contradictory on the surface, I didn't feel superior to anyone. I just felt spiritually—almost supernaturally—astute. I knew that I had seen a side of life that they probably never would. Unquestionably, if I had my choice, Bill would still have been alive and I would have been happy being spiritually ignorant and boring. But I didn't and, as a result, the world was so different than I once, not too long before, knew it to be.

The frightening thing about such an awakening is that this perspective can steer you in one of two directions. The first being that you become paralyzed with your newfound enlightenment. If you feel that nothing really matters, then it's easy to see no purpose in continuing to live. Even if you do persist, you may feel deluged with sensations of hopelessness, loneliness and purposelessness. How do you begin to move up and out from the bottom of the chasm of depression if all that you see, hear and touch is intrinsically unimportant? For the many that don't just wither, fall into a ball and die, there are still often bouts with alcohol and drugs. Such a person's definition of happiness consists only of feeling good again and not from their interaction with others, achievement of goals or pursuit of purpose. Even more develop deep pangs of anger, which grew from the death of the loved one and the helpless position into which they were involuntarily thrust.

The second direction one could take from their new position of enlightenment is to use the fresh perspective as a way to make their lives richer and more meaningful than what they may have originally set out to do. After the death of a loved one, I think people teeter on the edge of these two decisions, and depending on the support of the family and friends and the person's overall nature and contentment before the tragic incident, they are nudged onto either side.

My mother's insistence that we all move forward with our lives was, I believe, the initial push that allowed me to grow from Bill's death rather than wallow in and be consumed by it. I nurtured my healthy perspective through the support and love given by my family and, as a result, took the awful experience of Bill's death as an empowering force rather than a destructive one. I remember making a conscious decision to not let Bill die in vain, but rather to use his suicide as a beginning point for the rest of my life. I wanted Bill to still be teaching me things in some way.

In the book, *"My Son … My Son … A Guide to Healing After Death, Loss or Suicide,"* the author, Iris Bolton, recounts a conversation she had the day after her son, Mitch, committed suicide, in which a psychiatrist-friend of hers described the 'gift' that Mitch gave to them. The 'gift' was, as Iris came to understand, her newfound ability to use Mitch's story to help a multitude of others get through the loss of loved ones. While I'm not comfortable with the term 'gift', I understand the concept of what the psychiatrist was explaining and what Ms. Bolton came to find as truth. Bill's gift to me was my new perspective on life. At a very young age, I was able to understand what was truly important and began to structure the course of my life primarily around those things. While so much of life still focused on avoiding Death, I began to revel in the small moments that made up my day: conversations with my family and friends, the scene outside our windows of the forest and deer, fierce or perfect moments of the weather.

But only being away from Bill's death a few months now, the newfound perspective from his 'gift' couldn't help me to avoid the long road of healing that still stretched far ahead.

9

I have no idea if it was weeks or months, but I know that I slept in my parents' room for a long time. Every night, I contemplated sleeping in the room I shared with Bill and couldn't bring myself to do it. I had a hard enough time when I had to go in to retrieve clothes for each day, let alone actually spending an entire night in there. Our room was spooky, but the closet, in particular, oozed death. The rest of my house slowly drifted into a state of life, as Death gradually let go of its hold on most of the rooms. But Death was stubborn when it came to the walk-in closet that Bill and I shared and seemed to hover there like a cat standing proud over the mouse whose life it had just snuffed away. When I walked in, the air felt thick and cold, making it difficult to breathe. I was enveloped in fear, afraid that I would either hypnotically follow Bill's actions or see Bill standing there with death dripping from his skin, reaching out to touch me.

One of my recurring fears was grabbing what I needed from the clothes rack, turning around and finding Bill, gray and sorry, between me and the closet door. He'd want to stop my exit in order to help me understand what and where he was. I pictured him standing before me, half hunched over with the necktie dangling from his neck, his throat marred with a thick red ring just below his Adam's apple. His warm blue eyes would hold only blackness, while his skin lay on him, pasty white and cold. His voice would be strained, weighed down with distress and desperation. And I couldn't bear to see him like that. Whenever I entered the closet, I stared straight down at the floor worried that my nightmare would come true.

At some point, I made my way back into the room that Bill and I had shared and slept in his bed, as it was the farthest from the closet door. But being in the room with that closet attached was brutal and I went to bed every night fearful of what would come out at me. Wanting even a false sense of security, I included checking the closet in my nightly ritual of going to bed. I'd flick on the switch, hold my breath and cautiously walk in, peeking first behind the row of clothes stretching across the rack at the back of the closet, then behind and under the dresser and beneath any pile strewn about. My heart raced, my forehead and palms poured sweat and every single muscle in my body tensed. These moments, more than any other, were the ones during which I most had to resist taking my own life. Death made it so easy, clearly displaying the clothes rack and ties similar to the one Bill used. It was inconceivably difficult not to follow Him, but I had to carry out the inspection regardless, unable to rest easy without it. When done, I raced out, slammed the door shut behind me and turned out the closet light with one final swat. If I missed the switch, I laid in bed, staring at the long thin beam of light at the bottom of the door, anxiously waiting for a shadow to break it.

I lasted in the room until the end of the school year when, like every summer, my family went down to our shore house in Ocean City, New Jersey. When we came back in September, my sister Suzanne left for her first year at Villanova and I asked my parents if I could switch rooms with her. Of course, they said that would be fine and I was in there the next night. I felt bad making Suzanne sleep in my old room whenever she came home, but I just couldn't hack it any longer. The new room—away from the closet and the mandatory, gut-wrenching inspections—was utter freedom for me and I found that even Death lost its power and suicidal seduction.

10

My family spent all of our summers in Ocean City, leaving our Schooley's Mountain home the day after I finished school and coming back the day before the next school year began. There was no place I'd rather be in the summertime (or any time for that matter) and I loved and appreciated the fortunate life I had. I went to the beach every day, swam or bodyboarded in the warm ocean, worked on my tan and developed some good friendships with the kids who lived nearby.

I don't remember much about the summer following Bill's death. I recall that I still played alone a lot and thought about and missed Bill tremendously, but being away from Long Valley was incredibly liberating. The negative energy of Bill's death seemed to blanket the air above the town. It infiltrated every tree, road, blade of grass, house and faraway mountain. Ocean City provided a great escape from this blanket of doom and when I was there, I felt more energized, renewed and safe.

The one thing I can unfailingly recall from that summer, however, is the first day I tried surfing. Bill surfed for a couple of years and had gotten good enough that my parents bought him a beautiful surfboard from a shop in California. Its bright yellow deck melted into a blood red bottom along the rails, while a classic raked, red single fin stuck out below the tail. I still remember him opening the huge box one Christmas Day and how its colors lit up the room (this board is the one on the back cover).

Before Bill died, my parents had always told me that I wasn't big enough or old enough to surf. As a result, Bill and I never had the opportunity to share waves together. While he rode all over the waves on the outside sandbar, I was relegated to the shore break on my bodyboard, riding the waves straight into the sand-lined shore. Occasionally, after one of my short rides, I stood at the water line with a hand above my eyes to cut down the glare from the sun, peering far out to sea, trying to catch a glimpse of Bill or his friend Gary sliding down some great wave. When one of them stood up, I cheered loudly, swiveling, twisting and contorting my body in anticipation of their next move.

Once in a while, when small-to-medium sized waves broke on the sandbar, Bill took me out on my bodyboard. Making motorboat noises (a loud engine revving sound as we went up the wave face or a slow drawn out brrrrrr idling sound as we cruised through calm waters), he'd put one hand on the front of the board and one hand on the back and push me from behind. I came to listen intently to the sounds he made to anticipate what was coming. Attempting to keep me in suspense, he'd slowly push me towards shore with the droning idling sound coming from his mouth, while he looked behind for the 'Wave of the Day'. When it came, he'd whirl me around without warning, belt out his revving sound and scream "Hold On! This is gonna be a big one!" Instinctively, I applied my best death grip on the sides of the board and yelled every time, "Nooooooo. We're never gonna make it over this one!" I'd feel his legs kicking furiously in the water and his strong hands holding fast to the sides of the bodyboard. The wave always loomed large in front of me and I never ever thought we were going to make it over. Laughing, Bill waited until we sat just below the falling lip of the wave before he gave one final strong push. I'd fly up the face and shoot skyward five or six feet. The wave would pass beneath me and I'd suddenly be even higher, feeling the exhilaration of flight. But then as I began to fall back towards the surface, I'd tense every muscle, bracing myself for the impending body slam, clenching my fingers around the rails and smashing my eye lids together until I splashed back into the water. Bill would pop up next to me, inevitably choking because his laughter prevented him from keeping his mouth shut, allowing salt water to pour in. Instantly, I'd relax my death grip and fall into the water, hysterical. As the waves continually rolled in, he'd insist I get back on the board immediately, since I would then be easier to keep an eye on. While kicking and splashing to get back on, I'd beg him to do it all again.

On the last day of the summer after Bill died, I was walking back from the beach when I passed his friend Gary waxing up his surfboard and getting ready to go out. Trying to help me out in what he could only imagine was an awful time, he asked if I wanted to grab Bill's board and join him in the line-up. "REALLY?" I yelled. "Yeah. Wait, I have to go ask my parents! Come with me, you know, to convince 'em. Please? Yeah!" I was excited because I finally had the opportunity to try surfing and because I knew in my heart that the sport would be bring me closer to Bill.

I practically dragged Gary over to my neighbor's house, where my parents and sisters were hanging out. Flying up the stairs, I found everyone on the porch. With fragmented sentences and short breaths, I explained that Gary wanted to take me surfing and it would be okay and I would be safe because he's really good and I get to use Bill's board. I remember Gary just nodding his head and occasionally interjecting things like, "Oh, yeah. He'll be fine." "No, I won't take him out in the big stuff." "Really, it's not too rough out there." Much to my shock, my parents thought it was a great idea and said they'd bring my sisters down to watch.

Gary and I went over to my house and grabbed Bill's board out of the attic. Lowering it out of the rafters, I could feel the scent of the wax still smeared on the deck wash over me and I could smell Bill once again. As we pulled the board out of the dank space and into the dark hallway, the yellow deck, though covered in dirt and dust, still shone brightly with the small red Bing insignia appearing illuminated. We got it outside and started to make our way to Gary's house to retrieve his board. I couldn't fit my arm around the wide, thick rails and so carried it with both hands, nearly falling countless times due to the excited pace of my walk and the size of my skinny body in relation to the board. But just having it in my arms made me feel as though Bill was nearby.

We picked up Gary's board and walked the half block to the beach. Along the way, I wondered if it would be hard for Gary to be surfing with me after he surfed with Bill and how lucky he was to have had that opportunity. While walking across the beach, Gary pointed to the waves breaking at a specific spot on the sandbar and explained where we would be surfing. The waves weren't big—only about three feet—but well shaped and consistent. He showed me the rip currents and how to avoid them and taught me how to mark my position with points on the shore. Reaching the water line, we stooped down to wax our boards when Gary suggested I surf the shore break for awhile before paddling out to where the larger waves broke. In the meantime, my family had made their way down to the beach and lined their chairs up in a row. Thick grey clouds covered the sky while not another soul covered the sand.

We put on our leashes, picked up our boards and walked into the warm September water. Gary paddled out to the larger waves crashing on the sandbar and, as promised, I stayed in the shore break. My family cheered me on and tried pointing out good waves for me to catch. Finally, one approached that I thought looked manageable. As Gary instructed me on the beach, I let it break and paddled furiously towards the shore, waiting for the rush of the whitewater to catch up and begin pushing me forward. When it hit me, the board picked up speed and glided towards the beach. Completely exhilarated, I jumped to my feet and rode it straight into the shallows where the large fin dug deep into the sand and finally stopped the board's forward motion. I leaped off, lifted my hands into the air and yelled, not believing what I had just done. I looked far out to the sandbar and saw Gary punch the air with a congratulatory fist. My whole family let out a huge "Whooooooooo, yeahhhhh!" while they held up signs that had numbers with their ratings of my ride like a group of badly dressed Olympic judges.

Invigorated, I immediately turned the big board around and pushed it back out into the ocean. With every ride, I felt more fantastic and closer to Bill. I longed for him to be out surfing with Gary on the sandbar and tried to envision him floating there watching me.

I rode the shore break for a couple of hours with my family cheering me on the entire time. As the sun began to make its final descent, Gary paddled up to me on his way to the beach and said he had never seen anyone get up so quickly. I was beyond thrilled and thanked him profusely as we both made our way to my family, now gathering up their things. They congratulated me, told me how great I looked and said I was a natural. No sport had ever given me the elation I felt at that moment, and I was only disappointed I hadn't tried it much earlier in the summer.

I was buzzing as we all walked back, as if an electrical current was coursing through my body. Not only did I have a blast surfing but, more importantly, I could feel the connection forged with Bill from the simple act of experiencing something he did and loved. He felt so far away then, but suddenly we had a life-line between us. Wherever he'd gone with Death, we'd somehow gotten a little bit closer.

The next day, my family packed up and made our way back to the lush, green hills of Long Valley. I always hated leaving Ocean City at the end of the summer, but this year was so much worse than any previous. I was leaving the one place in which I had felt safest since Bill's death. I had no idea how everyone at home would continue to react to me and still envisioned the town reeking of misery and sadness. And I was upset with the fact that I wouldn't be able to surf for the next nine months, leaving behind the only true connection between Bill and me.

My eyes filled with tears as we drove out of town and I noticed the sign on the side of the M.A.B. Paints Store that sat just before the causeway, leading west over the bay. It read, "We Hope You've Enjoyed Your Stay!" I listened to the rhythmic pounding as the tires went over the seams in the small drawbridge and looked at the bay as it stretched back towards the ocean with its long, slender blue arms. At the moment we reached the end of the bridge and pulled onto the Garden State Parkway, I slumped down in my seat and tried, without much success, to put away the feelings of doom that began to sweep over me.

When we arrived back home, the horrifying summer smells smacked me hard across the face. Death filled the house once again, and I hadn't felt Him as close during the past two and a half months as I did right then. My heart sank to my feet and I walked through the house with a renewed fear. I almost expected to see Death sitting in our living room, sipping a glass of cognac, laughing at us as we slowly made our way around. Once again, I had to summon up the energy to face Him and deal with His omniscient blanket of sorrow and sick seduction.

11

Around this time, my parents dragged me to see a counselor. Overall, I was doing fine, but they wanted to be sure that I had the opportunity to get out all of my feelings, thoughts and fears. In hindsight, I'm very glad that they pushed me to go, but at the time, I dreaded it. I had no desire to confront the pain that consumed my soul. We tried a couple of counselors before we settled on Father Baker, a priest/psychologist in a nearby parish. My visits were once a month.

My dread persisted the entire time I met with Father Baker, in large part because everything in the room in which we sat reminded me of Bill and his death. The air, reeking of burning candles and old wet rugs, brought me back to the church that housed Bill's funeral mass. The mahogany paneling, which blanketed all four walls, drew the color from almost everything in the room the same way Death stole the hue from all that surrounded my seat on the front stairs of our house the night Bill died. Even Father Baker's voice took on the sound that resembled the pain in my heart. It was a deep, normally soothing voice that caramelized every word that fell from his lips. If he were a late night radio talk show host his voice would sound groovy, soulful and pleasant. But in the context of our meetings, his voice rang only of sympathy and pity. Every time he opened his mouth, I was reminded of the horror of Bill dying and of the fact that I was so emotionally destroyed that I had to come and sit in front of some stranger who could bring me back to normalcy because he had acquired several, long-worded college degrees. Conversations never felt like the equal exchange of information they were meant to be. They felt forced, always driving towards some specific goal or point with little emotion from Father Baker. I wanted warmth and compassion, not analysis and objectives. As a result, I wasn't compelled to volunteer a lot of information. Basically, Father Baker asked me a question and I provided him with an answer. The session would last 60 agonizing, often upsetting minutes and then I'd be done until the following month.

In all fairness though, Father Baker was a huge help. He was able to awaken things in me that I had locked away. I came to understand the pain and sadness that had torn me to shreds. And I learned the role I had within the lives of my family and friends, that I needed to be strong not only to survive, but for them to as well. When my work with him finished, I knew that I had progressed further away from my grief than I would have had I not gone to him at all.

Towards the end of this stint with Father Baker, my parents decided to tell me the way Bill died. Up to this point, they had no idea that I knew. I never said anything to them, my sisters or even friends. In the beginning of one of our sessions, I was asked to sit out in the waiting room while my parents spoke to Father Baker alone. I waited in a dank room off of the reception area for what seemed like forever until Father Baker came out and said there was something that my parents wanted to tell me. When I followed him in, I instantly noticed that both of their faces were red and wet, smothered in tears that had been flowing for a long time. They both clutched tissues with my mother holding hers between folded hands and just below quivering lips. Frightened, they sat with their heads half-cocked and gaze cast downward.

I took the seat next to my mother with my father on the other side of her. My mom grabbed my hand, as tears continued to fall from her bloodshot, swollen eyes. Father Baker said, "There is something your parents want to tell you" and then nodded at them to reveal their deep, dark secret. My father looked at me, the floor and then at my mother. They glared at each other, their fear rising with every second. Sniffling filled the room until my father finally muttered, "Uh, Michael. We wanted to tell you that … Well, your mother and I felt it was important to tell you that Bill didn't have a heart attack. He … took his own life."

"I know," I said, at which I thought they were going to fall backwards off their chairs.

"But how? How could you know?" they both yelled simultaneously.

"Because, I heard Dad say 'Get the rope' when you went into our room and I just knew from that."

"But, you never said anything."

"I just figured you said what you needed to say. I just knew."

"We're so sorry, Michael. We just didn't know how to tell you. We …"

"It's okay." I assured them.

The energy poured back into my parents' bodies as relief swept over their tired, beaten faces. Their tears stopped flowing and their lips formed a slight grin, knowing that they had finally been relieved of their tragic secret. We talked a little more about the night Bill died, but didn't really get into any details about his method, if he left a note or how they found him. We talked about the drug situation at Smith Roberts, the stories the kids and the school bus driver had told them and the revelations those stories offered with regards to the amount of pressure continually thrust on Bill. We talked about the alcoholic principal, the mentally abusive wrestling coach and the students who seemed to funnel the most pressure onto Bill. Mostly, though, my parents just looked at me saying over and over again, "I can't believe you knew this whole time!" Father Baker sat frozen the entire session, and, to my recollection, never said a word.

The session proved to be an integral part of the healing for all of us. As I no longer had to hide the fact that I knew about Bill's suicide and my parents didn't have to keep their secrets locked away, we were able to talk more freely about Bill's death and the circumstances surrounding it. A greater understanding as to the possible causes spewed forth when the opportunities arose, and we began to ask each other questions without the fear of what the others did or did not know. Our healing, as a result, progressed faster than it had in months.

12

A couple of years after he died, Bill came back to me. It was only for a moment, but it was one of the most beautiful moments I've ever felt.

Like every all-American boy from the suburbs, I played Little League baseball. Especially after Bill died, the sport provided a great release for me and the extra push I needed to ensure that I remained social and outgoing. I used to pitch fairly well, despite my small stature and frame, but couldn't hit or field to save my life. Overall, though, I had a blast.

This particular season, the team was different than any for which I had previously played. Surrounded by a league of coaches who took the game far too seriously, our virgin leader, Mr. Jacobi, took over the reins with the only cardinal rule being that every kid plays in every game for equal time. He didn't care if one kid was a superstar or the worst player from the Bad News Bears. It didn't matter if we were in the first game of the season or in the bottom of the seventh of a do-or-die playoff game. Baseball was meant to be enjoyable and every kid would intimately learn that simple, oft-forgotten concept.

To further ensure that we had fun, Mr. Jacobi went to great lengths to establish a party atmosphere at each game by encouraging our families to come, cheer loudly and even make signs. My parents and sisters made a point of attending every weekend and more than adequately took care of the sign responsibilities. Because I could throw an extremely quick fastball (that often had an accidental, but advantageous curve), my teammates started to call me Zip. My sisters promptly made signs that read, "Zippity Doo Da Zippity Eh!" and "Go Get 'Em Zip!". They would even go so far as to sing the song—the whole song—as I was walking out to and back in from the mound. It didn't take long until all those in attendance routinely joined in.

The lightheartedness was further bred on the fact that we were the last team to choose our uniforms. Every Saturday, we played in the scraps left by the rest of the league; brown socks, grey shirts, orange hats and white pants. It was pretty tough taking ourselves seriously when we looked like an atrocious rainbow. I felt good on this team and a lot of my pain washed away when I took the field, heard the singing or basked in the all-around good vibes.

During the season, we occasionally played at Peter Carroll Field, a run-down, gravelly, dirt lot carved out of a mountainside. Behind the two teams' benches were steep pitches that climbed 100 feet, surrounding us like an amphitheatre. Beyond right field ran Route 514 while beyond left field lie another small down-slope and then the overgrown, brown, potholed parking lot. Overall, the field looked abandoned. But I always enjoyed playing there, as it was a refreshing break from the sterile fields we usually played on behind the school.

One day while I was covering left field (my contract must not have allowed me to pitch), I looked halfway up the slope that stretched behind our opponent's bench along the first base line. And there, by himself, looking back towards me with a slight grin and a complete look of contentment, sat Bill with his legs half bent in front of him and his arms resting on the tops of his knees. His brown, feathered hair was just as he had always kept it and his eyes looked soft and welcoming. He didn't acknowledge me, wave or say anything. He simply sat there, alone, taking in the whole scene. My eyes stuck to him and part of me thought that maybe it was just someone that looked a hell of a lot like him. But Long Valley was tiny and I had never seen this guy before (and never have since). I watched and no one went up to him nor did he go up to anyone. I remember dying to walk up and say, "Bill? Is that you? What are you doing here? I miss you so bad," but was afraid that he'd look at me and say, "Hey, I'm sorry man, but I'm not who you think I am."

The inning ended and I was over on the sidelines, watching him like a hawk, desperately trying to summon up the courage to walk up to him. But then, I looked away for a moment to do God knows what, turned back and found him gone. Had he actually been someone else, the set-up of the field made an easy escape impossible. I couldn't have missed him walking away. At the very least, I would have seen his car pulling out of the parking lot onto Route 514, but as keenly as I watched, I never even saw so much as a cloud of dust rise up.

When he left, I was shattered. I was desperate for any time with Bill, in whatever shape it took. Like a beggar grabbing at a piece of bread being held out by a pass-erby, I devoured the moment before me and longed for more. But I did acknowl-edge, even right then, that for the time he sat high up on the steep cliff face, I reveled in my feelings of safety and confidence. For those few minutes, I was secure with whom I was and that I would get through the terror that usually engulfed me.

The moment made me feel enlightened, strong and powerful. I don't know why I didn't become angry at him, demanding to know why he did what he did. I don't know why I didn't break down and cry when I noticed that he was gone. I don't know why, but the most natural reaction for me was to devour the good feelings and to make an extremely cognizant decision to use this moment to improve my life.

You may recall that on the day that Bill died, I had a game at Peter Carroll Field and, upon becoming agitated, Bill stormed away from my father and sat high up on the cliff face on the **left** field line. I actually didn't remember this until my father had told me just recently. I was dumbfounded and immediately relayed to him my vivid memory of Bill sitting up on the cliff face above the **right** field line. As the site of his final cries for help, my sighting of him was even more symbolic of why he came to me there. I was stunned when my father told me about that last day, and I cried like I hadn't in a long time.

13

After two years of therapy, I finally began to feel as though I was headed in a positive direction. At times, my days were still lonely, quiet, sad, and confusing. But with the encouragement of my family, I made an effort to rekindle my friendships and developed new ones. At the same time, however, Death still had a hold on me. While he was certainly not as omnipresent as He had once been, He could still fill me with a ferocious vulnerability. I wanted, more than anything, to push the fear from my head, to gain some sort of control. My immediate "answer" became the development of superstitions.

Now therapists call my superstitions a form of an Obsessive Compulsive Disorder or OCD. I became obsessed with touching things an odd number of times. When I closed a door, I had to touch the handle three times. If I brushed against a tree in the woods, I had to go back and brush against it twice more in the same manner. Even if I scratched my arm, I felt compelled to scratch it again at least two more times. I had to scratch my arm, touch the door or brush against the tree the correct number of times in the correct manner before I could move forward to do whatever I needed to do.

What would happen if I refused to perform these rituals, you ask? Well, as sure as the sun rises in the east and sets in the west, I would die. The idea was very real. I felt Death standing next to me counting the number of times I didn't do whatever it was I needed to do. I felt Him on my back and sitting on my shoulders, just waiting for me to mess up. I wasn't silly enough to think that He would take me out right there on the busy sidewalk, but I was convinced that He would take me while I slept or crash the car in which I was going to ride home. Because of my inability to carry out my necessary duties, my life would be over. That would be the last day that I would ever see my family, breath the air and feel the earth. And the worst part was it would be my fault. In my twisted view at the time, I saw my choices of touching or not touching an object the same as choosing life or death. If I chose not to touch the door handle or scratch my arm then I too was essentially committing suicide.

The superstitions were beginning to weigh heavily in my life. In many ways, this was an emotionally volatile period for me. I was content and able to socialize, but teetered on the edge between falling into a debilitating, compulsive nature or rising from the flames to continue my healthy process of healing.

During this time, though, the first of my synchronicities occurred. Looking back, there were certain moments in my life that changed the course of my thinking about and dealing with Bill's death. They came in many forms and always seemed to occur when I needed to move to the next level of healing, despite the fact that I may not have realized it at the time. Upon reflection, it appeared as though Bill would come to me at those times when I could have easily headed down a precarious road, put his hands on my shoulders and turned me the other way.

During one particularly beautiful summer afternoon, three years after Bill died, I was bodyboarding the small waves that broke out on the sandbar on our beach in Ocean City when I met a kid in town for just the day. We spent our time together riding the small, perfect waves and talking about where we were from and the things we liked to do. The fact that we began talking at all was actually strange, as I already had an established group of friends in Ocean City and would be hard-pressed to remember a time when I wasn't hanging out with one of them. My friends and I even used to make fun of the "day trippers" or "shoobies" as we called them, being a bit snobbish about the fact that they did not surf, live down at the shore or sport dark, even tans. But that day, I found myself enjoying his company and having a good time in the water.

At one point, I took off on a wave and tried to sneak into the little barrel that formed, but was denied even a moment of exaltation as the wave quickly closed out around me. Caught in the turmoil of the whitewater, I was driven down and rolled across the shallow sandbar until the wave finally released me from its grasp. When I surfaced, the board felt strange and I thought maybe something had happened to it during the pounding. I turned it over to take a look at the bottom and found that everything was fine. But when I flipped it right side up, my superstitions kicked in and I felt compelled to flip the board twice more. I thought it was completely inconspicuous, as the closest person to me was this day tripper 30 feet away. While I flipped the board for its third rotation, he yelled, "Heh! Was that a superstitious thing you just did with your board? I did that stuff for a long time too after my grandmother died." I was stunned and didn't respond. I stood mesmerized—shocked that there was actually someone else in the world that had done the same things as me in order to hold Death at bay.

As ridiculous as it may sound, up until this point in my life, I didn't think anyone knew what it was like to lose somebody let alone being consumed by uncontrollable urges. Everyone I came across seemed to possess such simple, basic, straightforward lives. It had all been so easy for them and they could never fathom what Death looked, smelled and tasted like.

In an instant, I no longer felt like the lone freak, tapping, touching and brushing things throughout my day. I realized that there were other people out there who knew the pain I felt and had similar reactions to it. Furthermore, with his words, "I *used* to do that," I had an example of someone who conquered the compulsions. The gates to my self-imposed hell cracked.

What's always amazed me is why I spoke to and spent time with the one kid on the beach who had experienced the same things I had and who had the courage and wisdom to verbally call me on my own paralytic behavior. There is no doubt Bill touched me that day, letting me know that the pain I felt was normal and that many other people have, unfortunately, felt the same feelings with which I was wrestling.

I don't recall talking to the kid after he uttered those words. All I remember is sitting on the blanket, staring at the ocean, completely unable to move. I sat there with my legs half bent in front of me and my arms wrapped around my knees. I was leaning towards the ocean, my head drawn forward and my back extended into a short arc, as the sun beat down on my tan brown skin. My eyes darted from the ocean to the sand to my mother, father and two sisters who sat around me reading their books or talking.

But I didn't feel scared or sad or depressed. I felt enlightened. I knew in my heart that what I had just experienced was an incredible moment of freedom. I felt the weight of the superstitions lifting from my shoulders and could, even then, see that day as the turning point in my struggle to break off the shackles the superstitions had fastened to my body. Bill sent this kid, I remember thinking, and it was such a wonderful moment whenever I felt spiritually close to him. It was from that position that I made the decision to grab onto these cataclysmic times in my life and use them to make me more wise and content. As I sat on the towel, peering out at the ocean, replaying that amazing moment in my mind, the world took on a new, fantastic hue.

I wanted to jump up and yell to my family, "Hey! You're not going to believe what just happened! I met this kid and he noticed my superstitions and …" But I knew there was no way to express the elation and enlightenment that filled my body. It's ironic, but writing this, I now realize that I felt *my family* wouldn't understand! I just sat there, reveled in the day and smiled.

Despite my elation, I still found that I couldn't stop my compulsions cold and continued to perform them in the weeks and months that followed. After we returned home from the shore, I decided that it was a good idea to go back to Father Baker to finally vanquish them.

Father Baker conducted his usual furrowed-brow analysis every other week and together we worked hard to free my young body from the prison that is obsessive compulsion. The sessions went on for six months until one day when I simply reached my breaking point. I decided—out of nowhere—that if I gave into the superstitions again I would die. And that was it. I used the fear of my compulsions to cut their power. Without question, I must have been ready for the transition and never worried again about tapping something in increments of three. I was free and it was fantastic. I walked into Father Baker's office for the next session and declared to him that I was now okay. I remember him sitting there stunned, leaning back in his chair and saying, "Well okay … wow … great!" I'm sure my mother still paid him his $100, but that was it.

It had been a long road that could have proven horribly debilitating. However, I was fortunate not only to have had the transcendent experience with the day tripper down at the shore, but also to have recognized it and embraced its healing powers.

14

I continued to work hard, staying social both in school and in the neighborhood. I participated in intramural sports and made an effort to play with the kids who lived close by. But I was still deep in the throes of feeling as though I were spiritually and mentally far ahead of anyone else in my life. Yes, I now knew that people like the day tripper existed, but most of the people with whom I came in contact couldn't fathom the anguish my family and I had gone through nor the battles I fought the previous years. As a result, I didn't get close to anyone outside the tight circle of my family. I often kept people close enough to count them as good friends, but at a safe enough distance to never have to rely on them for anything or miss them if they were suddenly gone. In fact, I grew quite proficient at this emotional balancing act. I'd built a well-protected structure around me that proved fairly impenetrable. On the outside, I was friendly and had fun, but inside I worked on shoring up the walls of my emotional vulnerabilities with everything I could gather. Sophomore year of high school, however, those walls began to flex when I met Emily.

We met for the first time at a mutual friend's birthday party held in Long Valley and I was blown away the first time I saw her across the room. She was the epitome of cute at an even five foot with shoulder-length blond hair, full cheeks and lips and big, round blue-green eyes. I desperately wanted to meet her and somehow managed to strike up a conversation. To my delight, Emily was as sweet, approachable and funny as she was beautiful. We hit it off instantly. When the night ended, I summoned up the courage to ask her for her phone number and then did everything I could to hide my shaking hands and the beads of sweat that ran down the sides of my face while she wrote the seven digits on a napkin.

We spoke for hours on the phone throughout the following week and conjured up any excuse we could to run into each other in school. Finally, after what seemed like the longest week of my life, we went on our first date—pizza and a movie. Incredibly nervous, I stammered through every sentence. While I didn't know much about dating at that point, I did know there was an intense energy between us. We easily fell into a relationship over the following months and I couldn't have been happier. I felt strong and confident when with her and, despite the walls I'd built to fend off my fears, fell madly in love.

Looking back, there were elements of our relationship that transcended the typical teenage infatuation. We respected and cared for each other to a level I've felt few times since and worked hard to continually show our feelings, actions that extended far beyond sex. In fact, while it sounds crazy given the context of our times, we waited quite a while before sex and even discussed it to be sure we were ready. But when we finally did take that step, it proved vital in further cracking the armor I had donned. By never taking it lightly, our physical relationship forced me to grow close to someone outside of my family and to risk the vulnerability that accompanies intimacy. Our relationship, on all of its levels, was what I needed to begin to reach out to the world again. Emily became the balance I lacked. She'd listen to my anguish and a moment later, shower me with the love and fun that came so easily to her.

Our relationship lasted through high school, college and two years beyond that, but our time together was inconsistent, riddled with break-ups. It was never due to any of the usual reasons that people walk away from relationships. We never lied, cheated or even got bored. We broke up, I realized much later, because despite basking in the strength and confidence she instilled within me, I couldn't put my demons to rest. Intense feelings of vulnerability occasionally rose from nowhere and placed the horror of losing someone I loved at the forefront of all else. In those moments, I ran. One day I'd tell her I loved her, the next I'd say, "That's it. I'm sorry, but I can't do this any longer. I just need to walk away." Every time, Emily would be dumbstruck and would just say over and over again, "I can't believe you keep doing this. You love me. Why do you keep doing this?" And in my heart and mind, I knew she was right. Yet, I couldn't conquer the vision I had of my world crumbling from the loss of someone else I loved and the place in which that'd put me. In order to survive, I subconsciously reasoned, I had to cut my emotional strings so that when the end inevitably came crashing down, I would have nothing remaining to lose. I remember sitting across from her, stone-faced saying those words yet again without even knowing why. I must have done this to her at least a half-dozen times throughout our years together. In the end, the trust and commitment we had to each other lay shattered in pieces by the constant fear that the end could always be just around the corner. We often tried dating again, but could never seem to do so with both feet on the ground. Over time, we drifted away.

Within a few years, we both met people with whom we became serious and our "on again-off again" relationship completely came to an end. We kept in touch, but only occasionally and always by phone. We both came to the conclusion that we wouldn't be together and moved on with our respective lives.

As it came to be, Emily was only the first in a long line of relationships in which I prematurely walked away. Actually, what first got me thinking about writing this book was my realization of my inability to keep intimate, close relationships. This realization came when I found myself in a bar with a girl I had broken up with months before. We were still friends and somehow got into a discussion that centered on the fact that I always bow out of my relationships too early. Frustrated, I wanted to understand what it was that drove me to do the same thing over and over again. I remember her leaning forward with this slightly incredulous look on her face saying, "It's because of your brother. You don't want to lose somebody again." And I knew she was right.

It amazed me that this fear could manifest itself in my relationships even up to 20 years after the fact. While I had given myself to all of these people—physically and emotionally—I had always avoided giving more of myself than I absolutely needed to. If I reached a level that required more investment of my trust and love, then I was gone. My actions flew in the face of all my mother had taught us. By ending my relationships early, I never got to know those people in the ways that I could have and in many instances short changed myself. But the realization also prodded me to take a look at who I was and to understand the full effect Bill's death had on me. I examined my relationships, my personality, my job and my interests. And everywhere I saw Bill's face. Sometimes smiling. Sometimes crying. All the time, having a profound effect on my life.

15

In high school, I decided to attend a retreat the Youth Ministry conducted annually for the high school kids in the parish. I wasn't overly religious and shied away from such events, feeling no desire to sit in a room and pray for hours on end while inundated with the smell of incense that reminded me so much of my time with Father Baker. But my friends who ran it insisted that the weekend was more about finding yourself than God and actually a lot of fun, so I gave it a shot.

The retreat began on a Friday night and ended Sunday afternoon at a house in western New Jersey. Much to my surprise, I didn't know many people when I walked in the door. There were a few who I knew from school and, of course, the counselors who convinced me to go, but that was it. Sharon and Phil, the middle-aged couple who ran the Youth Ministry welcomed us, briefing the group on the rules of the weekend and what we could expect. The 25 retreatants were randomly divided into groups of five and assigned two counselors per group. Breaking off into the various rooms throughout the large house, we introduced ourselves and talked about what brought us there and what we expected the weekend to hold.

The entire retreat centered around various talks given by the counselors—our peers. The topics included Family, Sex, Love, God, Choice and Relationships with content open to each speaker's own interpretation and experiences. Truly, this wasn't an overbearing religious weekend. God wasn't even present within most of the talks and the personal stories propelled us to think subjectively about what was presented. After each talk, we broke into groups to discuss our own perspectives. As mentioned, everyone had to share and, with the groundwork for honesty established by the speaker, our innermost feelings were easily brought out.

The retreat proved to be a major turning point in my life. It was the first time I found myself in an environment with other kids who encouraged me to delve deep into my feelings. While I still didn't think these people could understand my perspective, the counselors created an environment that allowed me to express my fears, joys and unanswerable questions. I cried a lot, feeling as though my memories and ruminations were finally given a proper release. It was intense. The communication filled a void that plagued my life for a long time, and I began reaching out. I even told one counselor he was the brother I had lost. I didn't want to replace Bill. I just hated no longer having an older brother from whom I could learn and pull from.

I was sad when Sunday afternoon rolled around and it was time to leave the comfort and peace of the retreat house and the people with whom I shared my pain. The weekend was important for my struggle back to normalcy and I couldn't fathom having to walk away from it. As we left, the outside world loomed large around me again and I felt, even perhaps more so than I had before, that I didn't belong. It was terrifying. But as my mother had taught me from the day Bill died, I had to venture out.

The weekend actually served two purposes. The first was for the youth of the parish to explore their emotional and spiritual sides in an environment not readily available to them. The second was for Sharon and Phil to recruit new Youth Ministers to the group in order to keep it strong and healthy. I was ecstatic when I found out about the recruitment aspect a week or two later. The retreat had been such a positive moment in my life that I desperately wanted to become a part of the experience from the planning side and offer to others the same sensation I had felt. I campaigned heavily with every counselor that went to my school and kept close tabs on when the final selection process would take place.

After a few months, I got a call from Sharon asking if I would like to join the group. She explained that it would be a tremendous amount of work and would require a great deal of my time, but that I should get a lot out of it. Without hesitation, I yelled "YES!" into the phone and told her how happy I was to have been chosen. "Well," Sharon said, "see you next Wednesday and welcome aboard." Upon hanging up, I flew through the house, finding my parents in their room. Relaying the conversation through heavy breaths, I told them how excited I was to join, asked if they minded driving me every Wednesday and rattled off the list of other counselors. Knowing how positive an experience the retreat had been for me and supportive of each step I made toward becoming the social person I had been before, my parents were pleased and encouraging.

The following Wednesday took forever to come, but at last I found myself jumping out of my father's car and heading into Sharon and Phil's house. Excited and nervous about what lay ahead of me as a counselor, I rang the door bell and slipped in when a chorus of voices shouted "It's open!" From the beginning, the environment was warm and inviting. The established counselors welcomed all of the new members with open arms, treating us as though we had been with the group for 20 years. After the initial re-introductions, Sharon reviewed what would be expected from each of us and laid out the agenda of events we would be organizing for the year. Then, as if it was just another meeting, she listed the upcoming activities, asked for various volunteers and threw out the evening's topic for discussion.

The events run by the Youth Ministry for the parish were anything from cake sales to dressing up as clowns for the local grade schools to the intense three-day retreat I had just attended. The group was hand picked and strove to reach out to the youth in the parish to get them more involved and to give them a positive base from which to build their confidence and self-esteem.

As mentioned, the second part of the meetings consisted of Sharon or Phil posing a question to the group. It could have been as straightforward as, "When have you been most scared?" or as unsettling as, "Have you ever attempted suicide?" Sharon and Phil would always share their experiences first to set the tone and direction of the answers. Then, going around the room, each youth minister would share his or her personal experiences.

I remember that first meeting and how taken back I was by the established counselors' incredible candor. It was amazing to me to see the older kids I looked up to, pouring their souls into the question without fear of reprisal or mockery. Their bare-naked execution of the stories that made up their lives inspired you to unveil your inner-most feelings; you knew that nothing you could say was stupid, soft or weak. The atmosphere was electric.

The initial meeting finished around 9:30 and according to routine, everyone carpooled down to Friendly's for ice cream, a late dinner or just some hysterical conversation. All 20 of us converged on the tiny restaurant and took the place over. At this point, our group wasn't about the secrets and sorrows many of us had just revealed. It wasn't about the ties we had to the parish or its youth. It was simply about a group of friends who shared a common experience, having a great time. In the initial outing and the many that followed, I laughed until I thought my chest would explode, traded barbs with anyone who needed a good ribbing and flirted with the female Youth Ministers. It was our way to release the emotion we'd just uncovered.

The selection process for new counselors was built around the idea of bringing in new people, who would not only work hard but provide a different perspective. Sharon and Phil didn't want a "Stepford" group of kids. They wanted a group that represented the town and was accessible to the kids of the parish on a very real level. We all had faults and were far from perfect. Patrick was a good-looking, albeit extremely cocky, womanizer. Sam was a hysterical, on-the-edge motorcycle rider. Jo was the beautiful, slinky, tight-clothed vixen. Mary was the cute, loud, I'll-say-anything-anytime tomboy. Ian was the dopey, mop-haired jock. Ed was the tall wiseass who wanted desperately to become the next great cartoonist. Heather was the adorable one with long brown hair and a breathy voice that often made people underestimate her intellect. Michelle was the slightly up tight intellectual from whom it was always easy to get a rise. Stewart was incredibly quick with a joke and could always be counted on for a snide comment. There were many others during the four years I was with the group, but these are the ones with whom I became the closest. It was an eclectic gathering of people, yet somehow it all worked and we all worked well together. Strong personalities sat next to passive ones, each feeding off the other.

In high school, I simply wanted to blend in with the crowd, keeping my unanswerable questions to myself. It was only in Youth Ministry that I could have been prodded into opening up about Bill as I did since I felt immersed within a non-judgmental, unconditionally caring environment. For the first time, it wasn't just me looking at the world mesmerized by the waywardness of it all, feeling as though I would never belong. Youth Ministry, and the retreats in particular, provided me with the method with which I could take my horrible journey and warped perspective out to the world to create something positive. By the time I left the group to go to college, I found that I had progressed far from the person I was when I first became involved. Youth Ministry gave me the next step in my healing. And it was a giant leap.

16

By sophomore year in high school, my relationship with surfing became an all-out love affair. Around this time, my parents bought me a full wetsuit that allowed me to venture out into the ocean from Easter through the beginning of December. As a result, I was in almost every weekend and my skill level jumped considerably. The more I did it, the more I wanted to and it transcended into a vital facet of my life.

There was rarely a time when I wasn't thinking about surfing. I dressed, head to toe, in the latest authentic surfer clothes and shoes. I wore down my tape decks with music from The Beach Boys, The Ventures and any other band that even so much as mentioned the ocean. My bedroom walls and school locker were plastered with pictures of waves, bikini-clad women and famous surfers. My notebooks and textbooks were covered with crude drawings of perfect waves breaking across the page and popular quotes from the current surf magazines like, "Surfing is like Sex. It feels good no matter how many times you've done it"; "Rippin' and tearin' J-Bay, Pipeline and Rincon;" and "Surfing is Life. The rest is details."

Before long, I became known in my high school as one of the only true surfers. Since we lived two hours from the nearest stretch of beach, this set me apart from the crowd as much as the empowered feelings born from Bill's death. I felt as though I was able to tap into something—the ocean enshrouded in its mystery, power, beauty, vibrancy and wonder—that none of the other students could even begin to comprehend. I gravitated to the sport as much for its athletic demands as for the individuality it fed my character.

But most importantly, I found that surfing still provided me with the strongest direct connection to Bill that I could ever have hoped to find. I missed him every day of my life, but I missed him even more in the water. The ocean became one of the few places that I could emotionally and spiritually feel Bill. As a result, I always felt safe and secure when I became immersed within it. While big waves scared me and I had definitely experienced the ocean in incredible bouts of fury, I never thought anything could happen to me while I was within its grasp. Bill would simply never allow it.

In the water, I often lapsed into thoughts of how my life would be different if he were still here. Would we have surfed together? Would we have owned a surf shop? Where would we have traveled together? How would he look? I thought a lot about how happy he must have been sitting in the water, waiting for waves, watching the sun rise over the dark blue-green surface. I pictured his eyes getting larger in anticipation of the swells rolling towards the beach and how his stocky frame stood tall upon the same board I was riding and slid down the waves' faces. I wondered why these moments weren't enough to sustain him and if he now missed them.

In many ways, my surfing was a sad reminder of what I had been through. But the beauty around me—the blue sky with dashing birds, the smooth waters with fish constantly breaking the surface, the sun, the beach, the sand and even the pesky crabs that snapped at my toes were all reminders of life and just how beautiful it was. Just the sight and sound of a breaking wave was enough to stir within my heart the deep passion that life can become. The scene was always amazing, and while it was a reminder that Bill was now only close to me here because he was in heaven, it was also a daily affirmation that life is so worth living if just for its natural beauty alone.

17

In my senior year of high school, Death once again drew close. But the frightening aspect of our interaction was not the fear I had previously felt or His seductive nature. It was my complete surrender.

One winter Saturday morning, Emily and I drove to a nearby college to swim at its indoor pool. We had a great time relaxing together, feeling as though we had gotten away from it all, even if only for a few hours. Deciding to call it quits around noon, we dried off, got changed and started driving back to her house. Approximately 10 minutes into the ride, while concentrating too heavily on signs that served to detour us around a construction area, I ran a stop sign. We were only doing 30 mph, but another car hit square into Emily's door at just over 50 mph. The impact pushed her door half way into her seat. My car flew across the road bouncing off a tree and then a telephone pole. When it finally came to rest, the impacts had shattered every window, collapsed the roof, dented both sides and propelled the trunk and hood open. Even both axles and the front grill were torn off from a cable half buried on the shoulder of the road.

My brush with Death came just after the initial moment of impact. When I saw the oncoming car, my vision blacked out. I could still feel and hear everything, I just couldn't see. I heard the screeching of brakes and the bellowing of horns, the sadistic crunching of metal and the shattering of glass. My head whipped in one direction, my body in the other, finally settling into a momentary weightlessness as the car flew across the road. The moments between the impact of the car and that of the tree appeared to stretch forever and somehow became peaceful. I remember thinking, "Well, this could be it. This is where it all ends and this is how you'll die." And strangely, that was okay. I was content with listening to the sounds the metal and glass made, as the car continued on its course across the road to smash into the tree and pole. I wasn't scared or even anxious. I have no idea why, but if I had died right then, my reactions were telling me that it was okay.

When the car came to rest, I regained my vision and found people swarming around asking if we were alright, what hurts and how much. Feeling a pressure on my right shoulder, I turned to discover Emily motionless, leaning against me. Blood fell in a steady stream from her head, contrasting sharply with the blonde curls that hung down below her chin. Her body slumped against mine like a discarded rag doll, her right arm still across her stomach. I screamed her name, while shaking her, but could get no response. Her head only rocked back and forth. I thought I had killed her and wanted nothing but to die at that moment. She lay like this for what seemed like a full minute and then slowly awoke groggily answering the questions that were fired at her from three directions.

I stepped out of the car and had only a couple of cuts and bruises. Emily had a concussion, a sprained ankle and several deep cuts from the glass that fell on her. The people in the other car were fine. All in all, we were very lucky. The police, those who rushed to the scene and the judge in court later all expressed shock that we came out of it alive.

Unquestionably, the accident frightened me and I was sickened to know how close I had come to seriously hurting Emily. But what bothered me as much was the intense feeling of calm and surrender that overtook me while we slid across the road towards the tree and the pole. I gave up fighting for my life when the moment arose to do just that. I don't know why. I don't know if it was from dealing with Death right after Bill died, thoughts that Bill was waiting for me or what, but the moment felt as though my time may have come and as young as I was, that was okay.

Please understand. Outside of this particular moment, I still feared Death. I no longer had the urges to commit suicide as I did in the closet, but Death petrified me. At those random moments when I would try to conceptualize what death was, I'd shudder with terror when I thought of my mind, heart and senses all ceasing. I shook with the realization that no one would see me any longer nor I them, and of the vision of infinite blackness overtaking my eyes. As a result, my calm during the heart of the accident was more disturbing to me than the accident itself. My reaction was the complete antithesis of what I would have predicted it to be. I would have thought those moments, in the car, sliding towards the tree would be one of the worst experiences of anticipation a person could have. But in measures of tranquility, I would be compelled to say that they were some of the best I have ever felt. There was a comfort there, but in what exactly I don't know.

18

As soon as I graduated high school, my parents moved to Morristown, 30 minutes east, in order to cut down on my father's horrendous two-hour commute. We spent several weeks going back and forth from the old and new houses transporting the many belongings accumulated over 10 years in Long Valley. Over the last several weeks, Emily and I made frequent trips together to pick up whatever we could.

It was bittersweet to break away from the large white house on the hill with the brick front. Bitter because it was where I had grown up. While in that house, I had developed an extremely loving relationship with my family, nurtured several strong friendships and had many great memories of hiking in the woods or playing in my Little League games. Sweet, because it felt good to break away from the sadness the house still exuded. I constantly thought of Bill there and what he had done. Every time I gazed on the bedroom door, the walk-in closet or his red, brakeless 10-speed bike hung in the garage, I thought of how he was no longer here. The time had come to distance myself from the constant reminders.

During our last visit to the house, Emily and I were walking through, taking one final sentimental journey. We ventured into my parents' bedroom where I was surprised to discover that they had stripped their walls of all of the wallpaper, in order to paint over the scribblings that Suzanne, Colleen and Bill had covered them with when we had first moved in. They told me later that they felt much of what was written was too personal and they didn't want to share it with the new owners. Honestly, I can't recall most of the writing and certainly can't remember anything that would make my parents feel uncomfortable. What I do remember was that Suzanne, Colleen and Bill had drawn a huge postcard on the wall with messages to each other. The messages were mostly comprised of such adolescent ribbings as "Colleen is a butthead" or "Bill plays with dolls." Emily and I laughed hysterically and I recall being struck by the innocence and happiness splayed across the bare, glue-speckled wall. It occurred to me, standing there, that the drawings were from a time when everyone was happy—way before Bill had ever contemplated death. It was a time when the worst thing in the world was being called a "butthead" and even that, you knew, was nothing. I made a point of making a mental picture of what lay before me and proceeded to walk through the rest of the second floor.

There was nothing left in the house—no furniture, pictures or even scraps of paper discarded during the move. The house was devoid of anything that marked our long presence. Nothing, of course, except the sad air that still emanated from the room at the end of the hallway that Bill and I had shared. But I was doing okay on this walk-through, elated from the drawings I had seen in my parents' room and filled with the sturdiness that the long passage of time can breed. I was ready to go into the room to take one last look.

Swinging the door open, I found that the room possessed little of its old character. The single beds that had been tucked away into the opposite corners were gone, as was the dresser on which Bill had *The Last of the Mohicans* sprawled out on his final night. Nothing hung from the walls, not even the curtains that filtered the sunlight. The only things that remained were the walls themselves, the ugly black-white speckled carpeting and the closet door to which I hesitantly decided to go over.

Emily wasn't with me at this moment. I'm not sure where she was, but I know she was wandering around somewhere upstairs. I turned the closet door handle and pulled it open, half expecting Death or Bill's ghost to come flying out, much as I did in the weeks and months following the night of his suicide. I stepped in and was immediately blasted with the cold air that always filled this space. Instantly, I became uncomfortable. My palms filled with sweat, my breathing grew short and shallow. All over again, I felt as if I was just a flash from the grip of Death. But I was older and stronger. I could handle this, I thought to myself. The only things in the closet were the clothes rack and shelf, both of which extended the length of the back wall. I slowly walked over to where I thought Bill hanged himself and was immediately taken aback.

There, in the brown shelf, were eight small markings, resembling fingerprints, which I had never seen before. With four prints in each group, each set stood shoulder-width apart from the other. The paint had been removed down to the wood in remarkably bordered elliptical circles. They appeared as though they had been made from an inordinate amount of pressure straight down rather than rubbed.

My gut screamed that, in the final instants of his hanging, Bill must have desperately wanted to live. Clutching the wood shelf with his fingertips in a last ditch effort to pull himself upright again, he couldn't overcome the strength of gravity drawing his body forward, which caused the tie to tighten just enough to stop the air in his throat. His last second wish was a second too late. Within moments, Bill lost his grip, his fight and his life.

While not taking my eyes off the marks, I yelled for Emily to come in. As much as I didn't want to put her through the thoughts and feelings I was experiencing, I needed validation of what I was seeing. I needed her to tell me what she thought the markings were. Reluctantly, she entered the closet. I remember her sad, consoling eyes and an apprehension that dominates anyone who walks into a room in which someone has died.

"What's up?" she asked softly.

"Take a look at this. Its … where … Bill … well … died."

Stepping closer to the markings on the shelf, she said, "Oh, Michael."

"I think those were from his fingers. I … never…. noticed them before." I didn't want to cry and tried to act strong, but I hadn't felt how I was feeling at that moment in a very long time. Suddenly, I could feel Death peering over my shoulder, laughing at us as we examined the desperate prints stuck forever in the wood. Death sat above us on the shelf and stood behind us in the closet, blocking the doorway. He was everywhere. "What do you think? I mean … do you see them too?" I asked.

"Oh Michael … yeah." She whispered again.

"Could they be from him holding on, ya' think? Like … maybe … maybe he was trying to hold on?" I asked.

Emily nodded and wrapped her petite arms around me.

Soon after, we left the house and slowly drove back to Emily's. For the duration of the ride, I gazed straight ahead, stunned and slightly confused, analyzing how those eight small circles could have come to be.

But, it wasn't sadness or anger or horror I felt with this moment. It was empowerment. I felt Bill wanted me to see those marks and had waited until he thought

I would be able to handle the meaning behind them. As I was about to close the Long Valley chapter of my life, Bill wanted to send me off with the knowledge and realization that he, in fact, didn't want to die, didn't want to leave us. In the throes of his horrible mistake, he desperately wanted to live; he just didn't have the strength to pull his body back into an upright position. While this knowledge didn't change the fact that Bill was gone, it provided relief and comfort to know deep in my heart that he wanted to live—no matter how terrifying life was or how daunting he saw the road ahead, he wanted to live. And that felt wonderful.

19

After completing high school, in 1987, I went off to St. Joseph's University in Philadelphia. When I initially looked back on this period in my life, I didn't think there was much from which I drew for my healing. My time in college just seemed like a period saturated with a lot of fun and some difficult schoolwork thrown in for good measure. I met a lot people, made many friends and dated numerous women. I discovered drinking (sophomore year) and managed to party pretty hard (no drugs), particularly the last two years. But recounting my days there, I realized that there were several key things I found during my time that extended beyond the education, the newly forged friendships and the many relationships in which I became involved.

Going away to school allowed me to walk into an environment in which I could start fresh. No one knew whether you were a nerd, a jock, the class clown or the kid who lost his brother to suicide, and no one really cared. You could be anything and anyone you wanted. Although I felt relaxed and thrived in the atmosphere, I still got close to no one and rarely experienced any deep conversations or introspection among friends. I kept it light and was known as the funny guy who would stop at little with regards to pranks or innocent mischief. The rhythm of class and school work was easy to hook into and most of my time was spent hanging out with friends in their rooms, in the library, the cafeteria or out on one of the many grassy knolls that stretched between the dorms and academic halls.

I rarely mentioned Bill or his suicide, not out of shame, but rather to finally gather some breathing room from the tragedy. And that felt pretty good. Everything about Long Valley possessed some kind of reminder of either Bill or his final act. It was hard, in many ways, to move past the pain since it was so ever-present in every nook and cranny of that town. But St. Joseph's and Philadelphia, as a whole, gave me a complete respite from that painful environment—even more so than did Ocean City, as my time down at the beach was always limited to a lightening-quick three months. When I left Long Valley, I left behind the monkey that perpetually sat on my back. My parents' move to Morristown also ensured that even when I went home, it wasn't to the town that caused so much pain. Everything and everyone was new.

Philadelphia was also the first large city to which I had easy access. I ventured in often, exploring South Street, Penn's Landing, the multitude of dance clubs, the historic district and the small outdoor cafes and coffee bars. The city life, sights and sounds were new to me, and I basked in being in such close proximity to its pulse. One of the most important components was the huge array of art exhibits adorning almost every corner. I had always been fascinated with the arts, involved with music and often read books on great painters and sculptors. But I never got the chance to see these works in person. Philadelphia opened the art world to me, particularly with the vast collection and special exhibits within the Philadelphia Art Museum.

At least a half a dozen times during the school year, I would take the Septa train into the city and walk down Ben Franklin Parkway to the huge museum that looked like the Parthenon on steroids. Inside, the world's history unfolded before me with images of early Christian Art, Medieval battle scenes, classical portraiture, romantic Impressionism, radical Cubism, and bold Van Goghs. I loved every stage of the evolution of art and found beautiful imagery in every period on which I sat and gazed. I wasn't a pretentious art connoisseur. I just liked what I liked and enjoyed the moment when I found myself in front of an original Matisse, Monet, Van Gogh, Reuben or Picasso. I reveled in seeing for myself what made these paintings so attractive and famous.

My exposure to these works was important as I came to feel that the essence of art exhibited the emotion of life. At its core was the passion of the artist; the delectable possibilities of what the world and people could look like and the gorgeous composition of color, medium and shape that were used to define a particular moment. Each piece whipped up emotions within me, whether they were happiness, pain, sorrow, wonder, fright or humility. Within that often gaudy frame, paintings hold all that is essential to making the world look good. It is more than just snapping a picture of a particular moment. It is accentuating that moment with a mood or a perspective. It is Monet's gardens, which seem as though they will drift into the air and vanish like a light morning fog. It is *The Massacre of the Innocents,* which depicts soldiers larger than any human; mothers whose faces are distorted in agony and babies whose supple, rosy cheeks still exude innocence and peace despite the knife tearing at their insides. It is even Rembrandt's subjects who peer out of the shadows as if they have the most incredible secret that they just can't … well, maybe … no, they just can't tell you.

For me, these works represented both life's limits and its endless possibilities. And when I walked out of the museum and into the blinding sunlight, horns, rude cabbies and racism, I felt as though I could see just a bit more of the wonder and stunning beauty that this long trip possesses—both in its physical and spiritual sense. Art allowed me to see and feel the complete antithesis of the pain that had engulfed me all those years before and that had taken Bill away from us forever. It permitted me to encounter, at the most basic level, the joy of life and drove home the fact that Bill had left behind a great deal undone, unfelt and unexperienced.

I decided, while at St. Joseph's, to learn all that Bill had not, to feel all that he had not and to enjoy all that he had not. However, I wasn't living to fulfill Bill's lack of experience, I was living to discard my own.

20

When I graduated college, I began working in the same industry as my father, selling advertising for a medical magazine. My first job, for an ophthalmic publication, took me into New York City. Our offices were in the heart of Midtown, at 40th and Madison. This young, skinny, naive country boy from Long Valley, who swore he'd never work in the city, found himself in the epicenter of the most powerful city in the world. Despite my time in Philadelphia, I remember feeling overwhelmed by the vastness and danger that New York exuded. I had no idea what to expect. Would I survive my walk to and from the subway each day? Could I give the level of competency that the "best workers in the world" would demand? Would I be eaten up and spit out like some ball player's wad of tobacco? It all seemed so insane, so fast, and so endless.

The homeless greeted me each morning as I stepped off the train. Hookers said goodbye each night. People pushed and shoved their way in and out of the trains and subways, up against the counters of the cafes and through the doors of the hundreds of stores and skyscrapers that lined my route. Morning, noon and night, a solid mass of people moved at a maddening pace through the streets and sidewalks. It was easy to forget that individual people comprised that mass, as it exuded a coldness and independence one doesn't feel outside of the city limits. No one stopped to give directions, the time or to suggest a great restaurant or bar. The multitude of people just needed to get where they needed to go.

The street was awash in a blanket of cars, cabs and delivery trucks all trying to get ahead of the other—their intentions exclaimed with a constant scream of horns. The buildings were the most grand on every scale that I had ever seen and the restaurants had the best food I'd tasted. The bars and clubs were filled with the latest in fashion, the hottest in music and the most absolutely beautiful women on which I had set eyes. Around me, individuals raced, the city breathed and the whole world watched intently and learned.

To my surprise, I enjoyed and fed off the energy. Often, during my lunch hour, I'd go for long strolls, usually up Madison Avenue to 50th Street, crossing over to Rockefeller Center, back down 5th Avenue, through Bryant Park and back over to

Madison Avenue. With a quick pace and wide-open eyes, I'd cruise through this same route each week, always encountering something new, bizarre, hilarious or unbelievably sexy. A straight path was forbidden, as hordes of people stopped, darted, and shuffled randomly into and from every direction. Each block contained street peddlers on every corner, like bookends, selling newspapers, toy cars, watches and old magazines. In between, wealthy locals whisked past the hypnotized slow-footed tourists whose necks hurt from gaping up at the skyscrapers and who actually waited for the crosswalk sign to read WALK. The doors to the Louis Vutton, Gucci and Tiffany boutiques constantly spun. St. Patrick's Cathedral never ceased to amaze. The splendor of the most famous ice rink in the world at Rockefeller Center always screamed of romance. Power lunches were taking place in many of the large picture windows, with the hashing out of deals that would affect our every need and want. Early on, I realized that every science teacher I had ever had was wrong. The core of the Earth wasn't comprised of molten lava. It was made of the asphalt, concrete, glass, attitude, money, power and virile voltage that formed Midtown.

And it was in one of these moments, one of these instances of walking among the masses, the wonder and the pounding energy, that the first realization of Bill's *non-existence* hit me like a train crashing into a car stalled on the tracks.

One day, within my first year in New York, while walking among the crowd that packed the sidewalk, I was violently hit with the realization that despite the millions of people who surrounded me in this city and the billions who occupied our world—among all those faces and lives—none were Bill. None! The realization wasn't just a momentary understanding or confirmation of this fact. It was horrific, striking fast and without warning, mercy or compassion.

The moment began with the physical sensation of being punched in the face. I stopped in the middle of my stride, in the middle of the sidewalk, finding that I was holding my breath, my eyes wide, my arms down at my side. For a second, I wasn't quite sure of what had just happened and felt as though the entire world had slowed down for an instant. And then, I was swept over with the thoughts—the awful, painful thoughts—that despite the masses that engulfed me, Bill was nowhere in this world. He did not EXIST anymore. He was now only a thought, a memory, the subject of a wrinkled, sun-bleached picture that was crammed into the side pocket of my wallet. And no matter how far I would search for him, look for his face in the maddening crowds around me, I would never find him. He was "away," as one of his poems told me. For just an instant,

I thought about where he was, if he was happy, what Heaven was. But the moment was mostly about feeling horribly empty. It came with a rush and went almost as quickly, leaving me in its wake, walking slowly with a hint of imbalance and a deep longing for something that my heart knew would never be. My body felt hollow again, as if my organs and spirit had been scooped out and thrown away, and I desperately wanted to cry.

I wanted to step aside, lean against a building and just stop. Stop and regain my thoughts and to let the realization that Bill was gone sink in once again. But I was afraid to do it, as I feared that just stopping would only make me more deeply feel the pain that Bill was nowhere to be found. So, I just kept going, regaining my stride, holding back my tears. Each step was deliberate, but each one brought me further and further away from the sudden flash of horror and pain that had just consumed me.

At that point in my life, I felt strong and confident that I had healed from the horror of Bill's suicide. I felt far removed from that awful May Monday night. There weren't many things that still strongly affected me about his death. At least not to the point where I would cry or feel physically beaten and exhausted. But this moment and the few similar such instances that have since followed were brutal, wrenching and momentarily debilitating.

21

Two years out of college, enmeshed in my job and entrenched in the New York City scene, I was winding up the tethers of my relationship with Emily while dating virtually anyone I found attractive and somewhat interesting. I recognized my need to play the field and did so with a kind of controlled abandon. I met women on the subway, in bars, on the street and in my gym. There was rarely a month that went by that I didn't find someone different with whom I would go out to dinner or meet for a drink. I was having a blast, unconcerned with getting married or even settling down in a long-term relationship. That all changed when I met Karen.

I met her at Gold's Gym and was instantly taken away by her beauty and warm, inviting personality. After several weeks of pursuit, she agreed to meet me for a drink in a local, restaurant/bar. Nervous and excited, I got to the bar 15 minutes early and was horrified to find its tables and chairs stacked in the corner and sawdust blanketing the floor. Unbeknownst to either one of us, the place was shutting down for good the following day. The kitchen was closed and the only person left working was the bartender. I lamented about the first impression I'd be presenting, but had to wait until she came before taking her somewhere else. Within 10 minutes, the front door swung open and she walked in. For a moment, my jaw dropped, sweat formed in my armpits and palms and I smiled a big, dopey smile. She looked radiant. Her almond-shaped blue eyes fixated on me, a wide smile formed beneath and, around it all, fell her full, long blond hair. "Hey, how ya' doin'?" she asked.

"Great," was all I could muster, before sputtering out, "they're going to close tomorrow. Should we go somewhere nicer?"

"Well, we could. But I really need a drink. So, why don't we just grab one and go from there?"

"Okay…. ya' know I had no idea they were closing … I …"

"No worries. It doesn't matter," she shot back with a smile.

I felt the first-date jitters wash from me within minutes as her warmth and attentiveness put me at ease. As the time passed, I became entranced by her insatiable hunger for travel and her entrepreneurial spirit and the worldliness that such interests breed. I found that her perspective wonderfully complimented my own and could see how each would build off the other. Our interaction felt so natural. It was as if I had known her my whole life.

One drink turned into another and then another and then another. Without taking our eyes off of each other and not wanting to interrupt the conversation, one of us would motion to the bartender to fill up our glasses by just raising our fingers in a peace sign. Before we knew it, it was past 1:00 am and the bar was announcing its last call to its only two remaining patrons. Amazed, we finished our drinks and walked to our cars, both expressing our desire to see each other again. On the way home, I was struck with the realization that I had just met the woman I'd marry.

Karen and I began dating, quickly falling into the rhythm of seeing each other on a regular basis. Within a month, I cleared my slate of other women and decided to throw myself wholeheartedly into this relationship. While there was a brief nine-month break when Karen moved to California, we dated exclusively for the better part of five years, including the year that we were engaged.

Ironically, though, our relationship was plagued with Karen's overwhelming insecurity and deep terror of marriage. The victim of an unbelievably awful domestic situation, Karen allowed the brutal experiences to hold her within their painful grasp. Over the years, her confidence eroded and she was overwrought with an inability to live life on her own terms. While the signs for me to walk away from this relationship continually appeared the longer I knew her, I was in love with the potential of what I knew our union held. Despite the anguish we endured because of her turmoil, I really wanted it all to work. Our final downfall was the moment I asked her to marry me. Any confidence she still had in us was lost, replaced with the dread of having to confront her demons. Her reaction was "Shit! Shit! Shit! Shit!." She didn't tell people we were engaged for a long time and, despite the fact that we were together for another year, never even approached the setting of a date. As she became more consumed by her fears, I became more angry with the fact that they had never been dealt with. After a full year of intensifying exasperation and a loss of both ourselves and the relationship, we decided to walk away.

It has been years since our break-up and, at this point, I feel more compassion for Karen's paralysis back then than anything else. There was a time when I was angry, but I couldn't continue to hold on to those emotions and remain healthy.

As difficult as my time with Karen proved to be, I can't deny that the relationship was important for me for two specific reasons. The most significant resides in the fact that it was the first time I decided to confront my fears of losing those close to me and to throw myself headfirst into a relationship without looking for the EXIT signs. I had kept everyone emotionally at bay since Bill died and never felt what it was like to completely open my heart and soul to someone. I had gotten close with Emily, but always chose to run when any doubt reared forth. When I met Karen, I knew that I had to make the decision to either entirely pursue the incredible potential we had together or to walk away and always wonder. Choosing to immerse myself in our relationship made me feel as vulnerable as someone hanging on the end of a cracking branch. But as the days and months passed, I learned that I couldn't have experienced the happiness and enrichment that an open and loving relationship can create had I not exposed all of who I was.

While I saw many of the signs that our relationship was faltering, I stayed because I was afraid of repeating my long history of giving up and never allowing the relationship to fully run its course. When it all ended, I forced myself to dwell on the victory I experienced in defeating my fears, rather than the blindness they temporarily created.

The second reason our relationship was so important was because of the awakening I had when I finally walked away. Without realizing it, I had become an angry, virulent person. I lost myself in the struggle to make the relationship work and in the bitterness that finally engulfed it. The pain throbbed inside of me and the future, at least with regards to our relationship, lay in tatters. Rather than confront this new pain, I withdrew from my family and almost all of my friends.

After the initial shock of it being over wore off, I plowed through my inevitable grieving process. With patience and compassion, my family and best friends were all there to provide comfort and perspective. Through their support, I realized that by losing myself the way that I did, and becoming such a negative person, I acted contrary to what my whole life since Bill's death had been about. The final straw was when my best friend said, "Dude, you were such an asshole last year that I didn't want to hang out with you. You just brought everything and everyone around you down." It was one of those instances that brands itself into your memory. From that moment on, I decided to rise from this second tragedy to feel and live life again as I hadn't in the previous two years.

I began working out vigorously, dropping 25 pounds in a couple of months to become leaner than I had been since college. I traveled extensively, reaching Alaska, Hawaii, Maine and Ireland in the ensuing 12 months. I drew closer to my family and worked hard at building my most important friendships. I started writing this book. But most of all, I vowed never to allow myself to lose the person I was for anyone or anything again. The idea that this vow could send me back to those days when I was afraid of throwing myself into a relationship was not lost. For a time, I found it hard to give myself to the women I dated. But the more I lived life as passionately as I had before my time with Karen, and the more I stepped back and took a look at the predominantly negative elements that comprised our relationship, the more I was able to understand what made a good relationship healthy.

The rise from this second, but much more minor tragedy was vital in reinforcing the lessons that I had learned from dealing with Bill's suicide. And if that meant that I became even stronger, then I would feed off the pain our relationship created like I fed off the pain that Bill's death generated.

22

Around 1995, I had two more close encounters with Death and found myself, once again, suspended between a peaceful bliss and a horrifying reality.

The first occurred in early November when a hurricane had roared up the coast delivering huge, powerful waves to the Jersey shore. After a week of obsessively watching its progress on the Weather Channel, I awaited the storm's passage beyond our stretch of coast when the winds would come around to groom and perfect the enormous swells that poured onto the beaches. By Friday, the storm had passed New Jersey and began to head northeast, clipping the tip of Long Island. The winds were forecast to switch from the northeast (stormy seas) to the northwest (a smooth ocean surface) overnight. Saturday was THE day. I met Pete, my surfing buddy, at his house early the next morning. With our boards strapped down in the back, we jumped into his pick-up truck and bounded down to our favorite break in Manasquan. The timing of the storm couldn't have been better: Saturday morning (no work), mid-low tide (not too shallow), and a beautiful, warm, sunny, fall day.

A nervous anxiety filled me as we sped down the parkway. With my heart racing and hands shaking, I yapped about nothing the entire time. Finally, after an hour and a half of driving, we pulled into Manasquan and snaked our way through town until we turned onto the avenue that ran parallel and closest to the beach. The bulkhead teased me, obscuring my view of the ocean. Finding our parking spot, we barely let the truck stop, jumped out and ran to the edge of the sand to take a look. It was as I had hoped. Big, glassy waves stood on the small, defined sandbar and peeled forever with perfect, round barrels chasing the thick, green lips. It didn't get much better, particularly with no one else in the water. We hustled back to the truck, threw on our wetsuits, grabbed our gear and bolted back to the beach. While we squatted on the sand waxing our boards, the waves exploded, filling the air around us with sonorous booms. The darkness of the water and thunderous reverberations were daunting, but I had surfed waves like this before. I felt confident and secure as we strapped on our leashes, walked into the water and began to paddle out.

Surprisingly, the paddle out wasn't bad, as Pete and I easily made it to just beyond the point where the waves were breaking. Huge swells rolled in, organized in clearly defined sets. They were well-shaped and incredibly enticing. I decided to start out on a smaller one to get acclimated and then, when I felt ready, would move on to the set waves. Within no time at all, what appeared to be a small wave approached. I spun my board around toward shore and began stroking for it, drawing my arms through the water with as much force as I could muster.

As I paddled into the swell, everything seemed right. When I knew I caught the wave, I sprung to my feet and watched as the shoulder grew and stretched out tantalizingly before my eyes. I stood, boiling with anticipation for the drop, until I looked below my board and saw nothing but 10 feet of air. No beautiful green face on which to slide down—only air.

When the wave hit the sandbar, its power had caused it to jump up at an alarming rate, transforming the smooth green slope into a concave, heaving monster. In an instant, it became impossible to make it down. With nothing but air below me, I'd free-fall into the trough.

I decided to jump backwards off my board to avoid the perilous drop and let the wave pass. In doing so, I could get out of the teeth of this one and have a go at another that was perhaps more rideable. So, I leaped back over the top of the wave into the water, swam back up to the surface, turned to look for any incoming waves and realized I'd made a costly mistake. Behind the small wave I exited was another larger wave already cresting and about to break on my head. With no time to grab my board and "duckdive" underneath it, I took a breath and dove deep under the surface, hoping I could swim below the cascading lip. It should have been easy to swim through these waves, as the swells in New Jersey don't usually hold a great deal of power. Usually, one simply swims under the wave and pops out of the water behind it. Usually …

When I dove under, the wave broke with such force that the lip penetrated the water and hit me square in the back. The concussion pushed me straight down while my head and feet flew upward, almost touching … and I'm not that flexible. I was shoved in this position until I hit the bottom—15 feet down. At that moment, when I felt my knees hit the deep sandbar, I knew these waves possessed more strength than anything I had encountered before. But I was okay. I always trusted my abilities in the water, I wasn't out of breath and, by hitting the deep sand I knew which way was up. I rolled my feet onto the bottom, crouched into a fetal position and pushed off towards the surface. It took several long strokes to reach the cool, clean, fresh air and bright sunlight. Knowing I was in the impact zone, I immediately looked out towards the horizon to see if any other waves were coming. To my horror, there was another bigger than the last, feathering ten feet in front of me. I still couldn't get to my board and so dove underneath the pitching lip.

But again, the wave broke with overwhelming force and slammed into the middle of my back. Again, I was pile-driven into the bottom, as though a sandbag had been dropped on me from a fourth-story window. Having no opportunity to grab a breath at the surface and unknowingly getting the wind knocked out of me, I had little air left in my lungs. I was scared, but went through the motions of pushing off the bottom and stroking to the surface. The trip seemed longer this time and a bit more desperate, but I saw the light get brighter through the water and knew that air was close by. With a violent exhale and wild eyes, I broke the surface. But there was no time for elation. A third wave loomed above me that was clearly bigger than the previous two.

Fearing that my board was what was keeping me in the impact zone, I reached down to release my leash. I thought I could swim easier without it. But I found that the leash had already snapped and then noticed my board bounding in on the whitewater of the previous wave. Spinning around to face the next wave, I took a quick breath and dove under to escape its crashing lip. But this one gave me my worst thrashing yet. It flipped and twirled my body, driving me into the deep bottom for a third time. I was frightened, exhausted and out of breath. It took me a second to get my bearings and my chest felt tight, as if all the air in my lungs had been sucked out with a vacuum. My arms and legs were sore and my back felt stiff. The three beatings had taken their toll. The dark water that surrounded me offered no beauty from which to pull inspiration, and I suddenly wasn't so sure that I would make it to the surface. But again, I pushed off the bottom and slowly made my way toward the sunlight shimmering far above. I noticed that my movements were much slower and my lungs felt taut as the last bit of air escaped. Yet, somehow I stayed calm and kept working my body in the direction of the enlarging light. With little strength, I managed to break the surface, sucking in as much air as I could possibly take in with panicky, shallow breaths.

Shaking, I looked to sea to find the thick green lip of a fourth wave hanging over me like a hungry lion poised to pounce on its prey. With no time to draw a good, strong breath, I dove as deep as I could and prayed I would push through this one with little consequence. It was not to be.

I heard the wave crack the surface with the resonance of thunder, while simultaneously feeling its unbridled strength grab and twist, shake and roll my body with frightening ease, as if I was a bone in a pit bull's mouth. I was driven deep, but didn't hit bottom, which was worse because I didn't know which way was up. My lungs burned from the empty draw they pulled. I surrendered any notions of control I still brazenly held.

At this moment, a beautiful sense of calm overtook me. There, deep in the dark, cold water in the heart of the impact zone, on a bright sunny November day, I found myself accepting my own death. "This is it," I thought. "This is where I'm going out." Time seemed to slow and I no longer wanted to fight. I remember the coldness of the water on my cheek, the heaviness that took hold of my body and the enveloping black around me. I didn't want this moment to be my last, but when it seemed as though all hope was gone, I was okay with it. I didn't see my life flash before me, encounter images of Bill or even become scared. I just accepted what seemed to be the inevitable. In a surrealistic moment, I sat, suspended far below the surface thinking, "Do I even want to try? Do I even want to fight? I could just hang out here and quietly die. I could just stop fighting." But giving up wasn't an option and at this point I did think of Bill. Not wanting to join him just yet, I decided to swim in the direction I thought to be the surface. Panic or fear still hadn't entered the picture. I had simply made the decision to at least try to live. I was content that if my exhausted, empty lungs were to give out, if I could no longer move my arms and kick my legs, if I found my forward progress halted and my body sinking towards the bottom, I would have been alright. That was just the way.

Needless to say, I did break the surface, my lips grasping the air. Finding myself facing the shore, I spun around to see what else was coming and found a couple of smaller waves feathering, but still in deep enough water that they held back from breaking. I couldn't linger where I was and so swam towards the horizon with what little energy I could muster. Spotting Pete just beyond the feathering swells, I yelled his name and urged him to wait. He looked back and was, he later told me, stunned by my wide, fearful eyes and the urgency in my voice. He paddled farther out to give me a proper landmark for safety and waited until I reached him. I grabbed his board and floated there like a boat wreck survivor clinging to a piece of driftwood. He asked if I was okay and what had happened and then floated with me far beyond where the waves were breaking.

After 40 minutes, I regained my breath and much of my strength. Pete begged me to use his board to get to shore, but I insisted that I wasn't going to put him out as well. I assured him that I felt okay and asked that he just keep an eye on me as I made my way towards the beach. With that, I pushed off the board and swam. After 30 minutes, I managed to dodge the big sets and make it to the safety of the beach.

Upon retrieving my board, which had washed up a block away, I sat on the sand, trembling for over an hour and watched the huge waves smash onto the sandbar. With time to observe the patterns of how the waves were breaking, I realized that they broke far too fast to be ridden and that Pete and I had ignored obvious danger signs. I also knew that I had made the rookie mistake of taking the first wave of a set. It's a cardinal rule on big days to let the first few waves pass due to the fact that if you don't catch them or fall, you place yourself in the worst position imaginable—the impact zone. And that was exactly what I had done.

Safely sitting on the cold, soft sand, I was also overcome with the thoughts that my stupidity had almost cost me my life, and the thoughts of drowning in the cold, dark ocean filled me with nausea and fear. My calmness deep under the surface was most definitely what saved me, but my momentary surrender to Death's grasp was unsettling, as my life had become so wonderful. Giving up wasn't an option for me.

◆　　　◆　　　◆

The last moment I looked Death in the eye was shortly after the surfing incident. I had spent the afternoon riding a train from Washington D.C. after several days of business meetings. As the train made its way up the coast, a huge December storm thrashed New Jersey like few before. It had only arrived that morning, but by the time I reached the New Jersey train station 18 inches of snow had fallen. I always hated driving in the snow, transforming into a self-admitted pansy, but I was some 30 miles from home and figured I would just take my time, hoping the highways on which I traveled would be plowed. While the roads had, in fact, been maintained, the storm dropped more snow in less time than it could be cleared away. Several inches continually covered the roadway and now with nighttime in full force, the road surfaces began to freeze. With the traffic lines obscured, there existed a haphazard forward progression of cars with many stuck in embankments. Some spun uncontrollably onto the shoulder right in front of me.

After two hours of driving, I was finally within five miles of my home. While on a straightaway, I peered ahead in the distance to where it seemed as though the highway just stopped. All I could see was a solid path of white through the trees. Knowing that there had to be a highway there, I ventured on and within seconds discovered the root of the optical illusion. That portion of the highway hadn't been plowed for several hours, as the snowplows had stopped at the township line. I hit the unplowed stretch at 30 miles per hour and continued for another half mile, until the rear wheels of my small Acura Integra began to slip. Suddenly, the back end fishtailed to the right. I turned into the slide, but the rear whipped back towards the left like a pendulum. I turned the wheel again and brought the car back into the lane, but it continued its swing to the right. Fighting the pendulum effect was fruitless, but I tried to contain the car's slide at least a half dozen times. Finally, the back end swung 180 degrees, carrying the car backwards and sideways across the two left lanes. Since I wasn't going fast, it wasn't the oncoming crash into the guardrail that I was worried about. It was the eighteen-wheeler that had stayed approximately three car lengths behind me in the left lane. As I slid across the road, I looked at the headlights of the massive truck as it bore down on me. With its front grill now two car lengths away, I slammed into the guardrail and bounced back into its path. I sat there feeling like an ant looking up on a descending shoe.

As this realization swept over me, I was soaked in a soothing calm. I found those moments, staring up at the encroaching headlights, listening to the blaring horn and the roar of the engine, to be peaceful. Time didn't stand still and there were no white lights (except for those coming from the truck). I found myself bathed in a comfortable haze of death.

To my shock and relief, the truck squeaked by, literally grazing the driver's side mirror. I remember looking out my side window, seeing the middle of the wheel well and the bottom of the trailer gliding by within an arm's length until the final set of tires left my view. I couldn't believe my good fortune and sat stunned that all was in one piece. I began to shake as fear replaced the warm calm. The shudders sprung me from my shock, allowing me to notice an approaching jagged wall of headlights inching towards me through the snow. Luckily, they were still far off. Paralyzed with fright, I called my parents, desperately asking what I should do. "Get outta there!" they shouted back and then proceeded to talk me through the process of turning the car around and making the rest of my way home.

It was the worst half hour of driving I had ever done, but I made it back without further incident. Slumping down on the couch, I thanked God and Bill that I was still alive. I wasn't ready to go just yet.

The obvious commonalities between all three of my brushes with Death were that I truly thought I was going to die, and there were moments, smack in the middle of the experiences, that a beautiful calm overtook me. I actually felt good. Mentally, I was completely lucid, organized and calculated. Physically, my body felt relaxed, loose and light. I never clenched my teeth, screamed out or cried with fright. I had no whiplash, sore muscles or even deep bruising after any of my accidents. There was very little reaction at all. In all three instances, I succumbed to what I saw as probable.

And that was what scared me most about all of the experiences. I still have yet to figure out the significance of my sensations. But my gut tells me that my initial bouts with Death, right after Bill died—the sickening smell of the dirt, grass, flowers and trees; His dark presence in every corner of our house; His mocking laughter just barely audible as I lay in bed with my eyes wide open and my small body quivering—had hardened me and had wiped away the terror that Death once possessed. I had already seen the worst He could throw at me and little could shake me up again.

23

For as long as I could remember, my father and I had talked about going to Alaska for the ultimate father/son adventure. As my relationship with Karen finally came to a grinding halt, I found myself unattached and in possession of a fair sum of money saved up for things that would now not be bought. It wasn't hard to recognize that time as good as any for my father and me to fulfill our dream. He loved the idea and we immediately blocked out eight days for our trip.

Having no idea where to go to in Alaska, my father suggested I find a place with good waves. The trip could easily be built around surfing, as he was content with anywhere that offered decent hiking and fishing. After several calls to the various surf magazines and the Alaskan Tourist Bureau, we found the tiny, isolated town of Kijook tucked into a corner of the Gulf of Alaska. The literature and word of mouth promised consistent waves, bear-laden forests, an enclosure supplied by the second highest mountain range in the U.S. and fantastic salmon and halibut fishing. It had everything for which we were looking. After reserving our lodge and airline tickets, we anxiously let the year pass until we boarded the Alaskan Airlines plane in Newark, NJ.

On the plane ride to Alaska, I had finally begun to organize my thoughts for this book. For the previous two years, an internal battle raged within me between self-doubt and the need to charge ahead and simply do it. I knew that my objective and goal were good, but the fear that my perspective wasn't important and my life unworthy of a story paralyzed me. I needed to somehow know that people would benefit from what I had to say. I was immobilized to this point and had forced myself to start jotting down notes on the plane ride to Kijook, hoping that somehow that process would kick-start me into writing. But during the whole day of traveling, all that I could come up with were notes that revolved around the justification of my perspective. What I had was trash and the still persistent fear that this book would never come to fruition.

When we arrived, the place was breathtaking to the point that it looked fake—like the set of some epic Hollywood movie. Thick green firs spread out for tens of miles in every direction until they smacked into the bottom of a mountain range that exceeded even my most vivid imagination. The mountains, snow-capped and rocky from the base to the summit, sat blanketed in a soft pink mist, making them appear as only a reflection that might soon drift away. Eagles flew in the distance, while moose grazed at the end of the runway. The only people around were those who just got off the plane and those tending to it.

Getting our bags and rental car (a beat-up van with rusty water in the back and holes clear to the road throughout), we drove to the Mooring Lodge. Jessica and Brad, the young couple who ran the business, welcomed us in the driveway with food for breakfast the next morning (as the only store in town would be closed), fresh towels and toiletries. Their warmth washed over us within the first few moments of our introduction, and my dad and I immediately felt at ease with what we had gotten ourselves into. "Why don't you go in and get settled," Brad said, "and then Mike, if you want, I'll show you the surf spots before the sun goes down." Ecstatic, I agreed to the invitation. After we unpacked our gear and settled into the spacious and comfortable rooms, I climbed into Jessica and Brad's 4x4 and set out through the Alaskan rainforest to the beach.

Originally cleared by the military in WWII to protect the area from the Japanese, the road from the lodge to the ocean was in horrendous shape and driving was a slow affair. Constant rains and huge snows carved the dirt surface with deep potholes, while the road itself was an intricate maze of turn-offs, circles and dead-ends. Along with such sights as gorgeous expansive rivers and the wildlife, Jessica and Brad pointed out the visual cues essential to reaching the beach. They consisted of turning left at the "giant spruce tree," taking a right at the "cul-de-sac of mossy trees" or following the "path with the yellow flowers." All the while, I fired questions at them about the area, their lives and the surf. With the light fading, we pushed through huge puddles in the road whose water easily reached the bottom of our doors, overgrown thicket that made the road appear as a dead end and around the enormous trunks of fallen trees. We drove through low-lying areas of grass waving in the evening breeze, groves of towering spruce so close together that little light reached the ground and around rocky, unstable cliffs.

A half hour later, we reached the coast. The four good spots in the area were all within a mile of each other, and Brad and Jessica brought me to each one. The last spot, in particular, left me speechless. Fifteen miles out of town, with not a person or first aid kit close by, we parked high on a bluff overlooking the large beach and the cold Pacific, as perfect, empty waves broke on the shallow sandbar 50 yards offshore. I sat in the van overwhelmed with the realization that this area was the epicenter of the storms that deliver huge swells to Hawaii each winter and that I would be immersed within its waters the next morning.

After five minutes, we had to turn around and begin the drive back through the forest before it got too dark, which would have made the road and puddles difficult to navigate. And this was not country in which a person wanted to break down or get stuck, particularly at night. Three people in a van represented an easy dinner to the inordinate number of brown bears in the area.

That night, I excitedly told my father about the drive, the forest, the ocean, the beaches and all that I had learned about Brad and Jessica. I couldn't wait until the next day, I exclaimed, but also confessed to the nervousness coursing through my body. "Hey, see what it's like tomorrow. But I'm sure you'll do fine," my dad assured me. With that, we both staggered up to bed, bringing the long day of travel to a close.

The next morning I woke to my father nudging me saying, "Hey, come on! Wake up! You've got to hit the surf! That's what you're here for!" Seeing my eyes open, he drew the shades, letting the bright sunshine stream onto my face. I squinted and sat up in bed as he yelled, "Let's go! There's waves out there!" Swept over with the realization that we were in Alaska and I was about to get in the water, I sprang out of bed and threw on my sweatpants, a long sleeve T-shirt, a hooded sweatshirt and my favorite wool baseball hat. I was still nervous about surfing such an isolated, powerful break, but was also as excited as that first time I stood up on that warm September day years ago. While my dad went downstairs to put together a quick breakfast for me to take on my drive, I gathered up my towel, wax, leash, surfboard and wetsuit, which included gloves, booties and a hood. When I came downstairs, my father threw me the keys. I put everything I had into the van and ran back inside, hoping to move him along. He handed me my breakfast in a small brown bag and asked if it was okay if he hung back at the lodge. He was still exhausted from all of the traveling the day before and just needed to catch up on his sleep. He assured me he'd be back on track that afternoon. While I would have loved to have him join me, I didn't want to push him too hard.

"No worries," I said.

"And be careful!" he replied.

"I will."

As I pulled out of the dirt parking lot and onto the road that squirreled its way to the beach, I remember being struck with the realization that this was *the* moment. I was about to jump into an incredible ocean, deep in the heart of Alaska, alone with no recourse. I giggled, shook with nervous tremors and sang at the top of my voice to the awful 80's pop music crackling out of the radio.

Punching through the thicket and plunking through the Hyundai-sized potholes, I slowly retraced the roads that Jessica and Brad had shown me the night before. A couple of wrong turns and 45 minutes later, I finally made it to the top of the bluff that overlooked the break. With a rare blue sky stretched above, I looked on big, perfect waves peeling down the sandbar, groomed by an offshore wind. Much to my delight, the water was almost turquoise—the antithesis of the gray, metallic hue I expected it to hold. The bluff itself was a hundred feet high, its slope to the beach littered with enormous cedar trunks discarded by the colossal winter swells. Between the massive, smooth trunks lay the broken fragments of branches, small cobblestones and boulders. In the throes of such a beautiful, sunny day, the scene before me was the only indication of just how cataclysmic the ocean can get during the heart of winter.

While keeping an eye on the waves, I anxiously put on my wetsuit, waxed up my board, closed the door to the van, and threw the keys on the ground next to the front tire. I made my way down the slope of the bluff by walking from trunk to trunk to boulder to trunk onto branches to another trunk, until I made it to the beach below. Stooping down to put on my leash, I watched as a good set broke across the sandbar in just the right fashion as to allow for a long ride. The only footprints on the beach were those I had just tracked and large paw prints that wandered away from me in a drunken pattern. This was it. With some angst, I walked into the water, hopped on my board and paddled out through the impact zone.

After a few minutes of observing the waves, I paddled for one that I thought was going to break well. As it lifted me to its crest, I sprang to my feet. The drop was quick and steep, but the wave broke without flaw. I surfed it for over a hundred yards, even squeezing in some maneuvers. When I cruised over the shoulder at the end of the ride, I immediately relaxed, knowing that I could handle what this day was going to throw at me. A huge smile blanketed my face, as I paddled back out to my original position. Reveling in where I was and in the simple act of surfing, I began to notice the world around me. Salmon, still making their way towards the rivers, darted through the faces of the unbroken waves. Seals bobbed in the water, occasionally riding the swells towards the beach or smacking a salmon into the sky when they felt like a snack. Eagles soared down from a nest in a huge pine tree just to the left of my van to snatch the salmon the seals had missed. Far in the distance stretched the 18,000 foot St. Elias Mountain range. Every peak rose directly from the sea, and I watched incredible winds blow snow off their tops in monstrous explosions resembling clouds. I thought I was in the middle of a National Geographic documentary.

I surfed for three hours, basking in the solitude, wildness and awe that enveloped my heart, soul and eyes. I felt elated and alive. The stress of work, home and the failed relationship with Karen had finally washed from my body. Already, on that first morning, I had found what I had gone all the way there to find.

Tired and beginning to get cold, I took one last wave in and, for a few minutes, sat on the beach, leaning against a gigantic rock, absorbing the scene that lay before me. My muscles throbbed with the exhaustion of my workout and I felt wonderful.

Within a few minutes, I heard a dog bark and turned around to find Jessica and Brad's 4x4 parked behind my van on the bluff. Seconds later, Jessica and her daughter appeared carrying a couple of logs and a shopping bag down the slope to the beach. When I stood up, she yelled, "Hey there!"

"Hey," I replied while I walked towards them with my board under my arm.

"We saw you leave this morning and thought we'd come down to videotape you surfing."

"Oh, that would be great, but I've got to tell you. I'm wiped out and cold. I don't think I can go back in!"

"No problem," Jessica responded. "Why don't we light a fire and you can get some food in you?" At that, Jessica reached down into the bag, pulled out a beer, a pear and a Power Bar. It all looked better than any five-course meal at *Daniel's*.

While I ran up to the van and changed back into my sweats, Jessica gathered up some twigs and started a fire at the base of the bluff. Her daughter ran around the beach chasing the dog and occasionally throwing a stick in a game of fetch. After putting my board and wetsuit into the van, I negotiated my way back down the huge bank and sat on the log Jessica had positioned for me next to the warm flames now intensely burning. Immediately, the conversation fell into an easy flow about surfing, our homes, work and our families. Her round, brown eyes and devilish smile complimented her unguarded tone. She emanated positivity and a subtle desire for something more. I was struck by the sensation of talking with an old friend.

As I sat there on the log, enjoying all of her words and answering all of her questions, looking around at the beautiful scene that lay before me, I began to wonder why this woman drove 15 miles out to an isolated beach to share beers with a stranger. She didn't know me at all, yet trusted me enough to come out to a place that offered her no protection or recourse. She was exposed. Where I'm from, women don't put themselves in such a position. I became consumed with a feeling that there was something more that propelled her to this situation and felt some kind of connection being forged between us. But I couldn't put my finger on its source and while we continued to talk, eat and drink our Budweisers, I searched my mind for what this feeling could be.

Our conversation by the fire continued and my suspicious bewilderment grew. I was thoroughly enjoying our time, but couldn't pinpoint just what it was that we were doing. The conversation turned more serious as we both became comfortable enough to ask and answer more probing questions about our lives. Where our dialogue was going was anybody's guess, but it continually grew deeper and more intense. And then suddenly, as though we finally tuned in a song from a radio filled with static, the point of the conversation became clear.

I can't recall what brought it on, but Jessica mentioned that it had really been a tough year for her, as her brother, Sean, had died the previous November. He had been drinking with a buddy of his when, she explained, he started to joke around with what he thought was an empty gun. He put the gun to his temple, pulled the trigger and put a bullet through his brain. Her entire world, she told me, was destroyed. He represented so many things to her. He was not only her brother, whom she loved dearly, but also the lifeblood of Kijook. Incredibly good-looking, brilliant, charismatic and entrepreneurial (all adjectives reiterated by everyone else we spoke to), he was in the throes of establishing a solid tourism industry for the town that would revolve around fishing, hiking and surfing. He had built the lodge in which we were staying, had laid out plans for further expansion to accommodate the increased flow of travelers and began to look at ways to spread the word about this sleepy, isolated place that was passed over simply because travelers didn't know it existed. When he died, so too did all of his plans for Kijook. With a quivering lip and gaze that moved from my eyes to the sand or sea, Jessica painted a clear image of the devastation Sean's death had caused to her life.

As a gesture of comfort, I told her about Bill. Taken back, she sat looking stunned, her mouth wide open and her big, brown eyes tearing into mine. Leaning in as though she were afraid to miss even a single word that was said, she began to fire questions at me. Questions that would ease her pain and mend her heart. Questions like: How did your family deal with it? How did you get through the first year, the next and the next ones after that? Does the pain *ever* let up? Does the longing subside? Do you ever *swear* you see him? How did you become such a positive person after that…. you seem so happy?

I answered everything Jessica threw out at me and expanded wherever I could. I described my bouts with depression, my struggles with Death and my superstitions. I told her how my parents and sisters seemed to have dealt with it and how our cohesion as a family was what most got me through. I described the many synchronistic moments that had touched and changed my life. I told her anything I could think of that would help her. She sat there the entire time, looking at me with a starved impatience for solutions to her pain.

The beers continued to go down easy and it was, despite the sad content of our discussion, one of the most relaxed, enjoyable conversations I had ever had. Once in a while a tear broke through our eyes and our lips quivered with the recounting of the tragic days, the horrible longing for what was not to be or the memories of how Sean and Bill smiled, talked, walked or looked. The discussion grew larger with every answer, as though each reply was a building block in a tower constructed with moments of pain, love, compassion and loss. It felt good for both of us to share the intimacies of our lives.

Then, about halfway through our conversation, while staring into the flames, listening to Jessica's voice, I was struck with the realization that this conversation was why we were on this beach. That moment was, in fact, synchronistic for both of us. At just the right time in our respective stages of healing, something brought Jessica and me together on that isolated stretch of Alaskan wilderness to prod us to exchange the information for which we were both so desperate. Jessica reached out to me for anything that would prepare her for the days ahead. She needed to hear the pain I endured, my management of it and my rise back to living. She needed to see the reality of my phoenix-like journey—to put her hands around it, to touch, taste and smell it. For her to really move forward, she had to see that someone else had gone through the same experience and survived.

And this longing of hers, this desperate, insatiable need for which she pulled and tugged at me was the push I needed to write this book. How many other people like Jessica were out there, I wondered. How many others, who have lost brothers, sisters, parents, friends needed to hear my struggle in order to move forward? I knew, at that precise moment, that there was no longer any reason to doubt the importance of my perspective. It may not contain all the answers, but it could help someone nonetheless.

Realizing that I was within the throes of such a wonderfully enlightening moment, I became elated with the knowledge that Bill was touching me once again. I felt empowered like I hadn't in a long while.

Jessica and I stayed on the beach for hours until one of us had to get back for something—I don't remember what. It was a brutal feeling knowing that our conversation was coming to an end and for a few frantic moments, I tried to think of a way we could extend it. But it wasn't to be. I drove back alone through the deep dark forest feeling numb. The conversation played over and over again in my head while I unconsciously navigated the van through the nondescript turnoffs and swelled puddles. I was surprised when I found myself parked in front of our small lodge, not recalling any part of the ride. I felt strong and confident while I stepped out of the van, but as if I had just awakened from a long slumber. I tried to organize my thoughts to relay the afternoon to my father, but my mind wouldn't allow it. The only thing I could do was let the moment sink into my heart and trust my ability to explain it later.

Jessica and I saw each other a lot over the course of the week and unquestionably, an electricity passed between us every time we spoke or simply looked at each other. But we never again had the opportunity to sit alone to further discuss Bill or Sean and our lives since they died. When my father and I left Kijook, I knew that I left a great deal unresolved for Jessica and me. All I can hope for is that we can continually pull from that day on the beach and the magic it possessed.

24

By this time, I was deeply devoted to this book. I became obsessed, writing through weekends and on the train to and from work. I scoured book stores and the internet for information on suicide, depression and anything else I thought would be of help. Book after book filled my shelf and mind, but I wasn't quite finding what I wanted. Finally I stumbled on Kay Redfield Jamison's work entitled, *Night Falls Fast: Understanding Suicide*. It lent great perspective to my work, compassionately illustrating the horror of depression and what Bill's psychological state may have been leading up to his death. One of the most intriguing sections was one based on research that showed that social environments can greatly affect the serotonin levels in the brain, actually raising and lowering them depending on group interaction. If this was true, then it would provide one possible explanation as to what caused Bill's transformation from a nice, well-adjusted, strong individual to one who would make the decision to kill himself and then follow through. I reasoned that if Bill found himself in a social situation in which he felt isolated because he viewed himself as the only one not doing or selling drugs, as the only one who, while good at sports, didn't base everything on them and as the only one who didn't know *anybody* before going to Smith Roberts, then there was the possibility that his serotonin levels dropped, his body chemistry changed and he became depressed. He became someone who chemically lost the ability to reason, who could no longer see the many possible solutions available to him, who was powerless to battle the impulse to just die.

After I read the section by Ms. Jamison, I vowed to somehow find out more about the period surrounding Bill's death. I walked the halls of Smith Roberts, visited the gymnasium and traversed the campus. I went into the library and pulled the yearbooks from 1980 to 1984. I even copied down the names of the other kids on the wrestling team, the coaches and the faculty. Originally, I thought I would simply call the people on that list, but the more I thought about it, the more I wasn't sure exactly how I would react. Could I hold in my anger? Could I not beat them senseless? Could I not attempt to psychologically destroy them for taking away my brother? I wasn't sure and so thought it best to find the information I was seeking in another way.

But in the 20 years since Bill's death, I either found people who were unwilling to talk or who had very little to share. Another way never seemed to exist, and I wasn't sure where I would turn with my re-energized mission. But then Rebecca wandered into my life.

I met Rebecca while I was still in my "just dating" mode after my failed engagement. She worked in an arts and crafts store I used to frame the various pictures and posters I hung in my apartment. Struck by her natural beauty and quick, smart-ass wit, I found the nerve to ask her out for dinner. "Sure," she said. "Call me here at the store." Intrigued, I called her a week later, but never heard back. Figuring I waited too long to follow-up, I let her go and avoided going to the store for about a year. But then I found myself with several pictures from a couple of trips that I needed framed and ventured back in.

With my tail between my legs and a sheepish smile, I took the pictures to Rebecca's store. I was happy to find her still behind the counter and slightly surprised when I was greeted with a nice, albeit guarded smile. "Hey, Jen!" she yelled to her co-worker. "Surfer boy is back!" And with that the pictures were dropped off and I walked out of the store filled with a renewed intrigue about this unassuming, beautiful brunette. When I got home, I decided to play the odds and ask her out to dinner. "Sure," she said. "I'll call you at home later." Two days went by before she did.

We connected on that first conversation as though no time had ever passed and after a couple of more calls, decided to meet for dinner. As expected, we had a lot of fun. When I asked why she had never called me back when we first met, she replied, "Oh … come on. You were dating the world. I could just tell. And besides … so was I. It would have never worked then." I couldn't do anything but laugh.

Despite the many women I dated since my engagement ended, I hadn't felt an immediate romantic connection to anyone as I did to Rebecca. We spent quite a bit of time together over the course of the next few weeks and it felt great. I had even called up the other women I was seeing to explain that I found myself in a situation that I needed to pursue. The slate was wiped clean and I was throwing myself out there like I hadn't done in a long while.

Within a month of our first date, I helped Rebecca move into a condo she had just purchased. During the long day of packing and unpacking, her next-door neighbor, Tom, came over, introduced himself and promised to have a party on the next big snowstorm so Rebecca would have a chance to meet more neighbors.

A week later a huge storm hit. The highways were closed and local roads were to be used only by those trying to get home. While I detested driving in this weather, I felt inexplicably drawn to be with Rebecca and ventured out into the storm. In the areas where it wasn't snowing, freezing rain poured down. Several roads were closed due to fallen trees or power lines, while the others lay covered with slick layers of white. I crept along with the radio off, gripping the wheel and murmuring about my stupidity of making this drive for a girl. The usual 30-minute drive took an hour and fifteen. Relieved to make it without incident, I walked in her door, threw off my shoes, kissed Rebecca and plopped down on her couch.

True to his word, Tom gathered a few people in his apartment that night—five, including the two of us. After dinner, we went over with a bag of chips and a bottle of wine in hand. There were beers in the fridge, chips on the table and home-made brownies brought by one of the other girls. I didn't feel like drinking, so I grabbed a Coke, hung back and listened to the conversation. At one point, one of the girls asked where I had grown up. When I told her Long Valley, she replied, "I knew a guy named John from there. He had brown hair...."

"Oh yeah!" I answered while sarcastically rolling my eyes, "I know EXACTLY who you're talking about. John Johnson right?"

She laughed and said, "No, that wasn't it."

"Was it Brown, O'Reilly, Thomas, Baker, Levine, Reynolds, Johnson, Derrick-son, McLaughlin, Peters?"

Between gasps and laughter she said, "No, it wasn't any of those either. I'm sorry, I really can't remember."

Then, having no idea what my last name was, Tom said, "I went to high school with a Reynolds."

"Huh. What school did you go to?" I asked.

"Smith Roberts," he replied.

"Really. What year did you graduate?"

"'84."

"Well, you didn't know him all four years, did ya'?"

"Uh no. I only knew him my freshman year."

My face burned and my hands started to shake. I had always blamed every other student at Smith Roberts during Bill's period there. If I didn't know which ones pressured him, I would hold all of them accountable. "That was my brother," I muttered staring him in the eye. One could physically see the mental process of his putting two and two together.

He suddenly looked nervous, fidgeting with his pant leg. His voice shook as he answered, "That was the worst four years of my life. You couldn't even imagine how messed up that school was. It was a complete waste of my parents' money and of my time. It was just really screwed up." His reply backed up my initial impression that Tom was a nice guy. I decided to drop the conversation at that point and to come back and talk to him alone another day. Immediately, I went to the fridge, pulled out a beer and sucked it down. Within the hour, I had finished a six pack and half a bag of chips.

A few days later, I went to pick up Rebecca for dinner and knocked on Tom's door. When he opened it, his mouth dropped and he invited me in.

"Hey, about the other night …" I said.

"Yeah. That was pretty wild, huh?"

"Yes it was," I said as a smile drew across my face. "Listen, it was a long time ago and everything is cool now. But I'd just like to find out whatever I can about that time. Would you be willing to grab a beer one night and I could pick your brain?"

"Yeah, no…. no problem."

Tom met me a week later in a local bar. From the onset, he looked nervous as he tapped the table with his fingers, folded and unfolded his napkin and played with the straw in his Coke. Aware of the fear and discomfort that many people have about these kinds of conversations, I explained again what I was looking for. "When Bill died," I expounded, "I was just 10 years old and didn't have the means to talk to anyone about the school, his friends—anything that could help me. Even though you know in your heart that you probably won't ever find the reasons for why he did what he did, you just hope to stumble on something."

Tom nodded, adjusted in his seat and said he would be glad to shed any light on what I knew. To further break the ice, I brought up the odd set of circumstances that made him mention Bill.

"I couldn't believe I said that," he said. "When you left, I looked across the room at Stephanie and said, 'Shit, what have I done?' That was just too bizarre."

For the next couple of hours, Tom described the pervasiveness of drugs, the lawlessness at the school and the pressure that was exerted from all around. He told me what he remembered about Bill, the names of some of his friends and even of the girl on whom he had a crush. He said he was surprised when he had heard that Bill had committed suicide and was appalled when the school said it was an aneurysm. He painted Bill just as I remembered him: a nice, unassuming guy who, while quiet was social, built yet humble. He thought he was the farthest person from trouble as anybody could be. Our conversation proved enlightening and provided the basis for much of the information that is contained in the chapter on why Bill committed suicide. When it was done, I thanked Tom profusely for taking the time to talk to me. Not a lot of people are comfortable with such a discussion and, as I've found, many avoid it altogether. He told me that he was glad to assist and that he would try to contact anyone else from the school that he thought could help.

A few weeks later, Rebecca and I broke up. It was as though we both woke up one morning and realized we wanted very different things from the relationship. With little fanfare, we walked away from each other for good.

The synchronicity of our dating occurred to me in the days that followed. I realized Rebecca came into my life at the precise moment when I needed to understand more about Bill, his suicide and the effect his environment had on him in order to move the book forward and at a time when all possibilities were exhausted. Without her, I never would have met Tom. I couldn't help but think that Bill had touched me again, just when I needed him most. I was comforted by the fact that even after 20 years, he still had an eye on me and a hand on my shoulder, ready to turn me down the right path.

25

On August 17, 2002, I embarked on a 26-mile overnight walk from Annandale, Virginia to the Washington Monument. Organized by Pallota Teamworks to benefit The American Foundation for Suicide Prevention, 2,300 of us walked through the darkness of the night into the dawn to symbolize the birth of an assault on the epidemic of suicide and the stigma that often accompanies it. The walk was aptly named "Out of the Darkness." As a member of the AFSP for the past three years, I knew of the educational programs they created and of their overall mission and passion. I had spoken to their executive director, gotten to know some of their dedicated employees and, at one time, even pursued a position within the organization. I was ecstatic to participate in something that not only allowed me to actively take part in the fight, but to also do so for an organization in which I wholeheartedly believed.

I walked with my sister Colleen and a good friend of mine named Cindy. Participation in the event required raising $1,000. We mailed letters to our close friends and co-workers that explained the event and our reasons for doing it, while also containing a plea for donations. In all, I sent 25 requests. Despite the fact that I never specified how much I needed to raise, people responded immediately and with overwhelming generosity. I was floored by the amounts of money that poured in and the personal notes that accompanied many of the checks: "Keep up the Good Fight"; "It's just so wonderful you and your sister are doing the walk—I wish I could give you more"; "Good Luck and this is a wonderful thing you are doing." The one that most touched my entire family read:

Although I never met your brother, knowing you, I can only imagine what a tremendous loss it is for the world that he is not here.

I am sure that, wherever he is, he is REALLY proud of his little brother. I so admire everything that you are doing in his honor, and I hope that my small contribution will help you in your efforts.

The support from those who donated was overwhelming. I felt honored to have so many people putting their money towards a cause solely because it was important to me. While I had always been excited to participate, I found myself filled with an energy born from the responsibility to complete the walk—not just for the victims and survivors of suicide, Bill or even myself—but for the 20 people who were now behind me. All totaled, I turned in almost $2,000 the day of the event.

After months of raising money and training as best we could, the three of us found ourselves exploring the starting area—the parking lot of the Northern Virginia Community College—on the eve of August 17th. When we first arrived, I felt strong and relaxed. After taking in the mandatory safety video, Colleen, Cindy and I wandered around, grabbing last-minute supplies, joking about the task that lay ahead and assuring each other that we could do it without much difficulty. And while I thought of Bill, his suicide and the pain I had felt all those years seemed a distant memory.

People began to filter into the area. The participants started to fill a section of the parking lot cordoned off by two fences running parallel to each other, 50 yards apart with the stage at the far end. Family and friends spread sparsely along both fences, surrounding us on two sides. The power of the event didn't strike me until we wandered into the Memorial Tent in which we could write a short message on an enormous banner that would later be displayed at the finish line. Upon entering, I was struck by the large number of people crouched over, scribbling messages, trying to squeeze their heartfelt words in between hundreds of other notes—each message highlighted by a victim's name. Tears welled up in my eyes and I had to walk out. Escaping to an isolated portion of the parking lot, I paced until I regained my composure. Gathering my strength into a protective bundle, I walked determinedly back in, only to be repelled once again by the image of Colleen scrawling "Dear Bill" in a small pocket of space and of tears pouring from a photographer's eyes as she tried to record the emotion that engulfed the tent like fire. Again, I bolted towards the safety of my empty corner of parking lot, overcome with tears that now clouded my vision and smeared salt on my cheeks. After a few minutes, I harnessed the necessary strength to run back in and scribbled, "I love and miss you Bill" in one stroke.

When I walked outside, Colleen and Cindy were there waiting. "There you are." Colleen said. "I saw you go in and out a few times. What were you doing?"

"Oh, man I just couldn't handle it. Jeezus! I kept having to leave to get myself together."

We laughed hard and got away from the tent as quickly as we could.

With the start time approaching, the participant area became more crowded, while those cheering us on now stood two deep along the fence. Activity filled the air as people stretched on the ground, hugged loved ones and drank water in defense of dehydration. Anxiousness grew among the mass of people as the minutes ticked away and more walkers filed in. Standing amidst the energy, I took a moment to really look at those around me and, in an instant, was overcome by the realization that I had been engulfed by a sea of 2,300 other survivors. Around me stood thousands of people who knew the pain, horror and loss I felt for the past twenty-two years and who represented hundreds of individuals who took their own lives. Even more, every single person wore T-shirts or necklaces with their loved one's picture. Some even carried poster-sized prints on a pole, like Jesus carrying the cross. The images on the T-shirts were often supported by the victim's name and dates of birth and death. There were pictures of the young and old, of sisters and brothers, mothers and fathers and friends.

Each victim looked so strong, healthy and vibrant, smiling without exception. And yet every one of them dead by their own hand. Even after all I learned, I still found myself asking 'why'. Every vision of a victim and their survivors reminded me of Bill and my own journey. I cried whenever I looked around and found comfort only in staring at my shoes or the ground. While unfathomably sad, I also found the survivors and their accompanying images empowering, driving me harder to complete the walk. This was a greater mission than even I had realized.

After a short stretching routine and several speakers, one member of Pallota's team stepped up to the mike and delivered—passionately and robustly—the following speech:

I am alive …

> I may have lost my brother, my sister, my parent, my child, my friend but,
>
> I am alive.
>
> I am a survivor of the dark night of unspeakable loss, of my own darkness and
>
> I am alive.
>
> I am unwilling to stand idly by and allow shame to defeat love or silence to defeat action.

I stand for the enlightenment of a society that would hide from suicide and

I am alive.

I am unwilling for my perseverance to be in vain.

Unwilling for the passing of my friend to be in shame.

I loved them more then I loved myself and their life will have meaning in my action.

I am alive.

In a world blinded by the pursuit of pleasure, I am here to say that people are in pain.

In a world rushing to get ahead, I am here to say that people are being left behind.

In a world obsessed with the value of the market, I am here to speak for the value of life and

I am alive.

This will be no quiet fight.

I am the voice of audacity in the face of apathy.

I am the spirit of bravery in a world of caution.

I am a commitment to action in the face of neutrality.

I am out of the darkness…. I am into the light…. and

I am alive.

Those on the stage then marched down the stairs, through the middle of the crowd and into the night. The rest of us followed with tears soaking the ground beneath our feet and thousands of family and friends cheering us on.

Due to some logistical nightmares and one wrong turn that took us a mile out of the way (at the 22.2 mile mark no less), the walk took an agonizing 11 hours. We wound through national parkland, on the shoulder of busy highways and through quiet neighborhood streets. Along the route, everyone chatted, dissipating the fog of sadness that sat over us during the opening ceremony. The night was filled with complete strangers asking each other where they were from, their names and for whom they were walking. Throughout the crowd and throughout the night, these small, short conversations persisted, punctuated often by the thrusting forward of the survivor's T-shirt or necklace in an effort to bring the memory to one more person who understood the hurt. Instead of discussing the whys and how's, we celebrated the victims' time with us and the joy we felt doing this event.

The route itself was thinly lined with family and friends throughout the night, further thickening on the approaches of each rest stop (12 in all). A half-dozen dedicated spectators made it a point of cheering us into each one—no small feat, considering the event began at 7:00 p.m. and ended at 6:00 a.m. Except for the few secluded areas, there was always someone clapping, shouting out some inspirational message like, "You look great!" or "Only a little more to go!" Others handed out snacks and water they bought with their own cash. Still more people shouted from the windows of passing cars, complementing their encouragement with blasts from the horn. But the one bystander I can vividly picture is the man we passed at 4:00 a.m. His immense frame seemed to rise far above the crowd; his barrel chest and muscular arms dwarfed any body around us. Only able to see him from the waist up, I became fixated on his slowly clapping hands, the smile that spread across his face, and his soft voice repeating "You guys are my heroes" over and over again. It wasn't until I walked by him that I noticed a card table set up with a picture of a young boy—no older than 12—surrounded by candles. As we walked past, Colleen and I looked at each other and both began to sob.

At mile 22, we were held up so that we could walk into the finish line together. The last four miles were arduous (particularly with the accidental detour). We pushed ahead trying to block out the blisters, nauseous stomachs, and pulsating muscles that contracted further with every step. Slowly, the Washington Monument drew closer through the dawn, until finally we could see the finish line up ahead. The last half mile was jammed with family and friends, screaming at the tops of their lungs. My father appeared from out of the chaos, grabbing Colleen and I in one swoop while showered in tears. My mother waited at the finish line. Again, I was overwhelmed by the amount of people, by the thousands touched by suicide and the support that rained down on every walker. Again, I could only look at the ground, my lips quivering, my eyes filling with tears. We walked through the throngs of people, across the finish line and towards the stage that sat between two fences perhaps a hundred yards apart. As in the beginning, we stood in the middle while the spectators encompassed us. They stood four and five deep, filling the air with screams of happiness, pride, love and released anguish from years of hiding the truth. I looked around so as not to miss the moment, but found it difficult to do so for long, instead staring back at the ground. Thousands of survivors surrounded me. Some walked through the night, others made sure to be there to applaud our efforts. All of them, sporting the pictures of those they loved who had committed suicide. "Too many" I kept thinking. "Far too many."

Colleen, Cindy and I held hands throughout the closing ceremony at which a slightly different version of the "I Am Alive" speech was delivered. Dirt, sweat and salt clung to my aching body while my throat burned, thirsting for more water and food. My emotions, wracked with exhaustion and the amalgam of thoughts that bombarded my mind all night, ran unfettered, forbidding me to know if I would laugh or cry in any given moment. But what I most felt was the thrill of being a part of the fight—to be one of the soldiers in this inaugural campaign. And while the moment certainly felt good, I came to understand later that the walk was also an important validation for me: I had survived Bill's death. I had triumphed over all of the horror felt over the past 22 years, and I was alive. I had not let my heart and soul die with Bill, as my mother had feared. I had thrived, loved and now fought back.

Of course, my life still stretches far ahead of me, and there will be moments throughout that will be trying. But the walk was the first time that I actually allowed myself to step back, take stock and be proud. And that is what I thought Bill would be happiest about—not just that his brother fought the fight, but that he made a statement for life.

26

It has been a long, often difficult trip, but I've survived. When I read back over all that I've written and think of the scarred lives that many other survivors lead, I'm somewhat surprised to find I've made it this far, to a point of strength and happiness. That frightened 10 year-old boy—who was afraid to go to sleep, withdrew from everyone for a long time and suddenly found a world in which nothing mattered—seems like someone else. It scares me to see how isolated I became, how terrified, neurotic and filled with pain I was. How close I came to dying mentally and, particularly in the immediate period following that May 5th night, physically.

Obviously, there's still pain in my heart, as there always will be, but it's a different pain than in the years directly following Bill's death. It's no longer as sharp or as frequent as it once was and I don't feel as consumed by it every day, as I did for so many years. Death hasn't hovered above me like an eager vulture, and I no longer feel powerless in His grasp or drawn to His idealized romantic beauty. The only time it feels present is when the heat of summer mixes the scents of the trees, flowers, grass, dirt and rock into its agonizing potpourri. Yet even then, I'm not reduced to paralyzing fear. It simply hurts because it's the final sensual reminder of Bill's last night.

Overall, I'm proud of the person into which I've developed and proud of my ability to grow from Bill's death rather than to be destroyed by it. I'm confident in myself and in the decisions that I've made along the way, regretting little and as time has passed, fearing less and less. My world is no longer one of daunting darkness that threatens to squash me unless I can gain control. Rather, it's one that constantly amazes, fulfills and nurtures me with its inexhaustible supply of natural wonder and experiences. Undoubtedly, my notion of life has evolved far from the fantasy of escaping away to that deserted island in the Parliament cigarette ad.

I've also found that I now enjoy the warmth and support of my relationships rather than becoming consumed by the fear of losing them. As a result, I'm closer to my family than I've ever been, have several fantastic friendships on which I can rely (in addition to a multitude of acquaintances) and have felt the pleasure of throwing myself headfirst into a relationship. There are still those times when the vulnerability of losing those dear to me is almost overwhelming, but I'm no longer willing to sacrifice the joys of that relationship for the dread that it will one day no longer be. To continue shutting people out of my life or to supply only a glimpse into my heart would be to continue to deny myself further growth. And the focus of this entire journey has been to continually grow.

But, of course, the road isn't paved with roses and I'd never want you to believe that everything comes easy now or that I'm completely over the effects of Bill's death. The healing process is continual and, unfortunately, never-ending. There are things that I think about and do that I've had difficulty moving beyond. The first is the transience with which I see my life. I save money in mutual funds and a 401K. I look towards the day when I'll have a wife, kids and four-bedroom house. I try to plan out my career. Yet, I find it almost impossible to see myself here in 10 years, five years or even one. The suddenness with which Bill left me has never exited my heart and on a conscious level, I'm aware of how close I am to being erased from this world. I'm often anxious about the things I want to do, as I fear that I won't be around long enough to enjoy them. Many nights, when I lay down to sleep, I ask Bill for more time. Time to enjoy my family and friends. Time to see my nieces and nephew get just a bit older. Time to surf great waves just once more. In a way, this fragile feeling is good as it pushes me to achieve some of the things I may never have achieved, but I recognize that it is, on some levels, unhealthy. I want to reach a point where I enjoy the anticipation of what will happen in the future, rather than be concerned that the future won't come. While I have been successful in partly removing this fear, it has been stubborn. All that I can do is keep pushing on.

I also recognize that I'm anxious about leaving a mark on this world. I take stock of what I have and note the things that I've achieved in both my work and personal life, but I know that I don't allow myself the moments of acknowledgment that I should. I'm fearful of settling in to an anonymous life that will leave nothing of value to the world when it's done. In the years directly following Bill's death, I remember being struck with the understanding that many people had no idea that Bill had even existed. They had no idea that the brother who had taught me almost everything, who I loved with all my heart and whose death had completely annihilated the world as I knew it, had ever been here at all. And I remember how empty that made me feel. In all the ways I wanted to be like Bill, I never wanted to be forgotten.

I don't know what my mark will ultimately be or even if I'll have the power to bring it to fruition, but the pursuit burns inside. In an effort to foster its growth, I search for inspiration in everything I can, whether it be a book that has caught my eye, an exhibit, a program on television or a simple conversation with someone new. I'm most attracted to people's stories and am fascinated by not only their accomplishments, but also their abilities to rise above the faceless masses to place themselves in our collective consciousness. I'm hoping to understand their motivations and to find any commonalties between all of the lives I gaze upon, to see if there's something that I could use. No story is mundane and I pull from those of artists, entertainers and activists as much as I do from those of politicians, athletes and business executives. At the very least, my search has exposed me to a multitude of fascinating lives and information. Will I ever find that for which I'm looking and will it allow me to make a mark? I don't really know. But there's no other option than to continue to draw as much from life as I can.

The story I've shared with you is but a snapshot of my life as it is right now. Because we never fully heal when we lose someone, our lives and the way we view them are constantly evolving from the point of our tragedy. I may look back years from now and find that some of my perspectives have changed. That the fears I have now have been washed away or that new ones have arisen. That I've either taken great strides forward or have somehow been left standing in the same place. The people we meet, the places in which we find ourselves and the experiences that happen around and to us often uncover aspects of our journeys that we never thought possible.

But the one constant is that I've worked at becoming stronger every day, because it lessens the pain and hurt of losing Bill and allows me to suck every ounce of joy from life that I can. And in our world of surviving suicide—any loss for that matter—that notion is victory. Take stock in your journey so far and note the moments that have helped you survive. You'll have a view of the world like few of those around you.

The journey gets easier. Just stay open to the moments of healing that fill your life and forever push to be stronger than your previous self.

Bill's "Note"

✦

All poems are taken from:
The Best Loved Poems of the American People
Doubleday & Company, 1936

Hold Fast Your Dreams

Hold fast your dreams!
Within your heart
Keep one still, secret spot
Where dreams may go,
And, sheltered so,
May thrive and grow
Where doubt and fear are not.
O keep a place apart,
Within your heart,
For little dreams to go!

Think still of lovely things that are not true
Let wish and magic work at will in you.
Be sometimes blind to sorrow. Make believe!
Forget the calm that lies
In disillusioned eyes.
Though we all know that we must die,
Yet you and I

May walk like gods and be
Even now at home in immortality.

We see so many ugly things—
Deceits and wrongs and quarrelings;
We know, alas! we know
How quickly fade
The color in the west
The bloom upon the flower,
The bloom upon the breast
And youth's blind hour.
Yet keep within your heart
A place apart
Where little dreams may go,
May thrive and grow.
Hold fast—hold fast your dreams!

—Louise Driscoll

Out of the Hitherwhere

Out of the hiterhwhere into the yon—
The land that the Lord's love rests upon,
Where one may rely on the friends he meets,
And the smiles that greet him along the streets,
Where the mother that left you years ago
Will lift the hands that were folded so,
And put them about you, with all the love
And tenderness you are dreaming of.

Out of the hitherwhere into the yon—
Where all the friends of your youth have gone—
Where the old schoolmate who laughed with you
Will laugh again as he used to do,
Running to meet you, with such a face
As lights like a moon the wondrous place
Where God is living, and glad to live
Since He is the Master and may forgive.

Out of the hitherwhere into the yon—
Stay the hopes we are leaning on—
You, Divine with Your merciful eyes
Looking down from far-away skies,
Smile upon us and reach and take
Our worn souls Home for the old home's sake—
And so, Amen—for our all seems gone
Out of the hitherwhere into the yon.

—James Whitcomb Riley

All to Myself

All to myself I find the way
Back to each golden yesterday,
Faring in fancy until I stand
Clasping your ready, friendly hand;
The picture seems half true, half dream,
And I keep its color and its gleam
    All to myself.

All to myself I hum again
Fragments of some old-time refrain,
Something that comes at fancy's choice,
And I hear the cadence of your voice:
Sometimes 'tis dim, sometimes 'tis clear,
But I keep the music that I hear
    All to myself.

All to myself I hold and know
All of the days of long ago—
Wonderful days when you and I
Owned all the sunshine in the sky:
The days come back as the old days will,
And I keep their tingle and their thrill
    All to myself.

All to myself! My friend, do you
Count all the memories softly, too?
Sumer and Autumn, Winter, Spring,
The hopes we cherish, and everything?
They course my veins as a draft divine,
And I keep them wholly, solely mine—
    All to myself.

All to myself I think of you,
Think of the things we used to do,
Think of the things we used to say,
Think of each happy, bygone day;
Sometimes I sigh and sometimes I smile,
But I keep each olden, golden while
    All to myself.

—Wilbur Dick Nesbit

Is it True?

Is it true, O Christ in Heaven,
    That the highest suffer most?
That the strongest wander furthest,
    And more helplessly are lost?
That the mark of rank in nature
    Is capacity for pain?
And the anguish of the singer
    Makes the sweetness of the strain?

Is it true, O Christ in Heaven,
    That whichever way we go
Walls of darkness must surround us,
    Things we would but cannot know?
That the infinite must bound us
    Like a temple veil unrent,
Whilst the finite ever wearies,
    So that none's therein content?

Is it true, O Christ in Heaven,
    That the fullness yet to come
Is so glorious and so perfect
    That to know would strike us dumb?
That if ever for a moment
    We could pierce beyond the sky
With these poor dim eyes of mortals,
    We should just see God and die?

—Sarah Williams

He is Not Dead

I cannot say, and I will not say
That he is dead. He is just away.
With a cheery smile, and a wave of the hand,
He has wandered into an unknown land
And left us dreaming how very fair
It needs must be, since he lingers there.
And you—oh, you, who the wildest yearn
For an old-time step, and the glad return,
Think of him faring on, as dear
In the love of There as the love of Here.
Think of him still as the same. I say,
He is not dead—he is just away.

—James Whitcomb Riley

Trees
[For Mrs. Henry Mills Alden]

I think that I shall never see
A poem lovely as a tree.

A tree whose hungry mouth is prest
Against the earth's sweet flowing breast;

A tree that looks at God all day,
And lifts her leafy arms to pray;

A tree that may in Summer wear
A nest of robins in her hair;

Upon whose bosom snow has lain;
Who intimately lives with rain.

Poems are made by fools like me,
But only God can make a tree.

—Joyce Kilmer

There Is No Death

There is a plan far greater than the plan you know;
There is a landscape broader than the one you see.
There is a haven where storm-tossed souls may go—
You call it death—we, immortality.

You call it death—this seeming endless sleep;
We call it birth—the soul at last set free.
'Tis hampered not by time or space—you weep.
Why weep at death? 'Tis immortality.
Farewell, dear voyageur—'twill not be long.
Your work is done—now may peace rest with thee.
Your kindly thoughts and deeds—they will live on.
This is not death—'tis immortalit.

Farewell, dear voyageur—the river winds and turns;
The cadence of your song wafts near to me,
And now you know the thing that all men learn:
This is no death—there's immortality.

—Unknown

The Child's First Grief

Oh, call my brother back to me,
    I cannot play alone;
The summer comes, with flower and bee,
    Where is my brother gone?

The flowers run wild, the flowers we sowed,
    Around our garden tree;
Our vine is dropping with its load—
    Oh, call him back to me.

◆   ◆   ◆

He wouldn't hear thy voice, fair child,
      He may not come to thee;
His face that once like summer smiled,
      On earth no more thou'lt see.
A rose's brief, bright life of joy,
      Such unto him was given.
Go, thou must play alone, my boy,
      Thy brother is in Heaven.

◆   ◆   ◆

And has he left his birds and flowers?
      And must I call in vain?
And through the long, long summer hours
      Will he not come again?

And by the brook, and in the glade,
      Are all our wanderings o'er?
Oh, while my brother with me played,
      Would I have loved him more.

—Felicia D. Hemans

Where Did You Come From?

Where did you come from, Baby dear?
Out of the everywhere into here.

Where did you get your eyes so blue?
Out of the sky as I came through.

What makes the light in them sparkle and spin?
Some of the starry spikes left in.

Where did you get that little tear?
I found it waiting when I got here.

What makes your forehead so smooth and high?
A soft hand stroked it as I went by.

What makes your cheek like a warm white rose?
I saw something better than anyone knows.

Whence that three-corner'd smile of bliss?
Three angels gave me at once a kiss.

Where did you get this pearly ear?
God spoke, and it came out to hear.

Where did you get those arms and hands?
Love made itself into hooks and bands.

Feet, whence did you come, you darling things?
From the same box as the cherub's wings.

How did they all come just to be you?
God thought of me, and so I grew.

But how did you come to us, you dear?
God thought of you, and so I am here.

—George Macdonald

Acknowledgments

Colleen: From my temper tantrums with a crab trap (eternally documented) to giving me an amazing nephew and two nieces—I am thankful to have you as my sister. And I couldn't be more proud of your current success.

Suzanne: As the adventurer of the family, breaking ground for the rest of us, I am grateful. My life w/out parental controls would not exist had you not worn 'em down. HA! Thank you for your support throughout our lives and thank you for Kathleen. I'm seeing an actress or aspiring singer like her mom.

Maurice: You're inexhaustible care for *everyone* around you amazes me and I've been thankful to be on the receiving end of it many times along the way. Thanks for the paintball shots to the ass, taking care of Colleen and the kids and always being there.

Bob: Hopefully you've grabbed a copy of this book while on the road with the band. Thank you for your friendship, advice on money, relationships et all throughout all the years and for navigating me into my townhouse (If anyone needs a mortgage broker ...). I finally had the scratch to be able to listen. But most of all, thank you for being a part of the family, good to Suzanne and raising the most beautiful Yankee to ever one day play the game.

Billy, Caroline, Claire, Kathleen: *Nothing* means more to me than you kids. You've made me proud, laugh and love deeper than I ever knew was possible. I will be your unwavering supporter throughout your lives and hope to be your confidant and friend til we're all old and gray. I can't wait to see the incredible people you'll all become. I love you with all my heart.

Sharon Naylor: Thank you for your invaluable insight on composing the proposal for this book and on the workings of the publishing industry.

Dennis Murray: I appreciate your copy-editing talents and the fresh eyes on the manuscript. Your suggestions helped shape the book to what it has become.

And to all those who read the manuscript and provided insight along the way. I was touched by the time you took to provide your perspective on the most important endeavor in my life. Many of your suggestions were instituted and all of your thoughts were valued. Thank You.

Bibliography

On Suicide

Alexander, Victoria. *In the Wake of Suicide: Stories of the People Left Behind.* San Francisco: Jossey-Bass Publishers, 1991

Alvarez, A. *The Savage God.* New York: Bantam Books, 1973

Bolton, Iris with Curtis Mitchell. *My Son ... My Son ... A Guide to Healing After Death, Loss, or Suicide.* Atlanta: The Bolton Press, 1983

Fine, Carla. *No Time to Say Goodbye: Surviving the Suicide of a Loved One.* New York: Doubleday, 1997

Hewett, John H. *After Suicide.* Philadelphia: The Westminster Press, 1980

Marcus, Eric. *Why Suicide.* New York: HarperSanFrancisco (HarperCollins Publishers), 1996

Redfield Jamison, Kay. *Night Falls Fast: Understanding Suicide.* New York: Alex A. Knopf, 1999

Shneidman, Edwin S. *The Suicidal Mind.* Oxford: Oxford University Press, 1996

Smolin, Ann C.S.W. and John Guinan, PH.D. *Healing After the Suicide of A Loved One.* New York: Fireside (Simon & Schuster), 1993

Styron, William. *Darkness Visible: A Memoir of Madness.* New York: Vintage Books (Random House, Inc.), 1990

Other Sources of Information and Perspective

Gelb, Michael J. *How to Think like Leonardo da Vinci.* New York: Dell Publishing (Random House), 1998

Hopcke, Robert H. *There Are No Accidents: Synchronicity and the Stories of Our Lives.* New York: Riverhead Books, 1997

Martin, Calvin Luther. *The Way of the Human Being.* New Haven & London: Yale University Press, 1999

Patterson, Stephen J., James M. Robinson and Hans-Gebhard Bethge. *The Fifth Gospel: The Gospel of Thomas Comes of Age.* Harrisburg: Trinity Press International, 1998

Redfield, James. *The Celestine Vision.* New York: Warner Books, 1997

Tzu, Sun. Translated by Thomas Cleary. *The Art of War.* Boston & London: Shambhala, 1988

van Gogh, Vincent. Edited by Irving Stone. *Dear Theo.* New York: Plume (Doubleday), First Printing by Plume 1995. 1937 Irving Stone

Associations & The Suicide Prevention Lifeline Phone Number

The National Suicide Prevention Lifeline, 1-800-273-TALK, provides access to trained telephone counselors, 24 hours a day, 7 days a week.

American Foundation for Suicide Prevention (AFSP)
120 Wall Street
22nd Floor
New York, New York 10005
Phone: 888-333-AFSP
www.afsp.org

American Association of Suicidology
5221 Wisconsin Avenue, NW
Washington, DC 20015
Phone: (202) 237-2280
www.suicidology.org

978-0-595-42681-2
0-595-42681-6

Printed in the United States
73816LV00005B/130-204